# Praise for *Steady S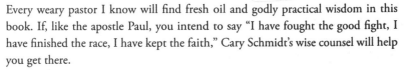

Every weary pastor I know will find fresh oil and godly practical wisdom in this book. If, like the apostle Paul, you intend to say "I have fought the good fight, I have finished the race, I have kept the faith," Cary Schmidt's wise counsel will help you get there.

**BOB LEPINE,** pastor, Redeemer Community Church of Little Rock; longtime cohost of *FamilyLife Today*

In most every conference talk I've done in the last five years, I've ended with an encouragement to stand strong for the journey. We need more finishers in ministry leadership. I'm thankful for this book. It's going to help us all with "steady strength."

**RON EDMONDSON,** pastor, author, podcaster

What if your setback, the adversity and discouragement you're facing, is God's invitation for something better? Cary Schmidt reveals a path toward healing for your heart, your relationships, and your ministry. This book gives real hope!

**CHRIS FABRY,** author and Moody Radio host

*Steady Strength* is soul food for any ministry servant. Cary invites us to examine ourselves for robotic habits that have crept into our lives, offering us biblical replacements for our mechanical inventions. The gospel has shaped both Cary and this book.

**FRANCIE TAYLOR,** author and president of Keep the Heart

In *Steady Strength*, Cary Schmidt calls those of us in ministry to a biblical and healthy definition of success. I found gems in every chapter!

**MARK HOOVER,** Lead Pastor, NewSpring Church, Wichita, KS

Beautifully blending story and principle, Cary has once again blessed us all with a read-worthy book. *Steady Strength* is refreshing, convicting, and sharpening and will prove to be a necessary resource for all Christian leaders.

**BRYAN SAMMS,** River City Baptist Church, Jacksonville, FL

Cary Schmidt always seems to know what I need when I need it. Like a timely vacation, this book refreshed and replenished me. Highly recommended.

**JEFF REDLIN,** pastor, Campus Church, Pensacola, FL

Cary is an experienced and trustworthy shepherd. The truths imprinted on these pages and applied to your life will serve to cultivate health for your soul and the congregation you serve. I invite you to join him on this journey!

**TIMOTHY R. SISK,** Professor of Intercultural Studies, Moody Bible Institute

Pastoral wellness is a topic that's been ignored for far too long. Cary Schmidt's book represents an amazingly thoughtful exploration of what it means to be a healthy minister of the gospel. It should be on every pastor's bookshelf.

**JONATHAN HOOVER,** Assistant Professor / Program Director, Regent University; Associate Pastor, NewSpring Church

For many years, Cary has been a tremendous example and encouragement to me in this area of sustainable, healthy rhythms in life, marriage, and ministry. I'm thankful that he has taken the time to candidly share his heart, his struggles, and his growth in this book for our benefit. *Steady Strength* will give you biblical truths and practical tools to get back up and soar again in God's slipstream.

**RYAN THOMPSON,** pastor, Liberty Baptist Church, Newport Beach, CA

Resist the urge to plow through this handbook for spiritual health. Take your time. Sit with Cary on the sidewalk of life and allow these words to slowly fill you with courage, joy, and strength. I recommend this book to all my preacher friends and fellow disciples.

**JOSH TEIS,** pastor of Southern Hills Baptist Church, Las Vegas, NV

As a pastor, I've experienced physical, mental, emotional, and spiritual depletion in my life and ministry. Thus, I'm excited to see the work Cary has done in developing a three-step model to pastoral wellness in his book *Steady Strength*. I truly believe this model has great potential to help any spiritual leader who needs *Steady Strength* to avoid the drift toward depletion.

**ERIC CAPACI,** pastor, Gospel Light Baptist Church; president, Champion Christian College

Cary Schmidt symbolically puts his arm around your shoulder, sits down with you, and reminds anyone in pastoral ministry what you need for the journey of shepherding God's people. It's a page-turner that will comfort, counsel, and cheer you on for the work God has called you to. Each chapter is a must-read! You'll no doubt, in the years to come, find yourself turning back through its pages and being encouraged again and again.

**MORRIS GLEISER,** evangelist, Rockwall, TX

This book is a powerful tool that will equip pastors and spiritual leaders for their daily calling. Well-written and encouraging, Cary takes you chapter by chapter through a journey of discovering where true strength comes from.

**JOSUÉ ORTIZ,** pastor and church planter in Mexico City

If you have found yourself believing that ministry exhaustion is the norm, that running on fumes is a sign of spirituality, or that ministry success is determined by the size of the audience, Cary offers a more healthy, biblical alternative. Ministry leaders can find steady strength by learning there's another way to be involved in gospel ministry.

**J. MICHAEL LESTER,** president, Veritas Baptist College

# STEADY
# STRENGTH

reversing ministry's dangerous
drift toward depletion

CARY SCHMIDT

**MOODY PUBLISHERS**
CHICAGO

Edited by Amanda Cleary Eastep
Interior design: Ragont Design
Cover design: Lance Schmidt
Cover illustration of mountains copyright © 2023 by Julia Korchevska/Shutterstock (393350029).

Library of Congress Cataloging-in-Publication Data

Names: Schmidt, Cary, author.
Title: Steady strength : reversing ministry's dangerous drift toward depletion / by Cary Schmidt.
Description: Chicago : Moody Publishers, 2023. | Includes bibliographical references. | Summary: "Ministry in modern society presents a perpetual assault on the pastor's soul. Yet far from a mournful manifesto of the burdens of pastoral life, this book is a celebration of the wonderful opportunity to shepherd God's people. In this three-part book, Schmidt unfolds an approach to sustained, joyful pastoral health"-- Provided by publisher.
Identifiers: LCCN 2023013908 (print) | LCCN 2023013909 (ebook) | ISBN 9780802431615 (paperback) | ISBN 9780802473202 (ebook)
Subjects: LCSH: Pastoral theology. | Clergy--Mental health. | Clergy--Health and hygiene. | BISAC: RELIGION / Christian Ministry / Pastoral Resources | RELIGION / Christian Living / Calling & Vocation
Classification: LCC BV4011.3 S383 2023  (print) | LCC BV4011.3 (ebook) | DDC 253--dc23/eng/20230705
LC record available at https://lccn.loc.gov/2023013908
LC ebook record available at https://lccn.loc.gov/2023013909

Originally delivered by fleets of horse-drawn wagons, the affordable paperbacks from D. L. Moody's publishing house resourced the church and served everyday people. Now, after more than 125 years of publishing and ministry, Moody Publishers' mission remains the same—even if our delivery systems have changed a bit. For more information on other books (and resources) created from a biblical perspective, go to www.moodypublishers.com or write to:

Moody Publishers
820 N. LaSalle Boulevard
Chicago, IL 60610

1 3 5 7 9 10 8 6 4 2

*Printed in the United States of America*

For my friend,

Don Sisk

At ninety years of age, with seventy years in global gospel ministry, nobody has more clearly displayed to me the joyful life of humble, faithful, fruitful service in the steady strength of Jesus.

Thank you for your steadfast encouragement, Christlike love, and joyful influence on my life and family.

# CONTENTS

# AFRAID TO FLY

*"He gives power to the faint, and to him who has no might he increases strength. . . . They who wait for the LORD shall renew their strength; they shall mount up with wings like eagles; they shall run and not be weary; they shall walk and not faint."*

Isaiah 40:29–31

There's a tiny feather stuck on the outside of the picture window in my breakfast nook. It's been there a few weeks, left intentionally to remind me of a traumatic morning I shared with a random robin.

It was about 7 a.m. on a pleasant fall morning. Beyond the picture window of our breakfast nook, the sun rose over the distant ridge. Fresh coffee in hand, I was forty-five minutes into morning study at our kitchen table when my frame of mind was rattled by a loud "thud."

*Oh no, not again.* A robin had hit the window. I bemoaned the death of yet another feathered friend. It's not uncommon to find the recent remains of an unfortunate flyer on our sidewalk.

I peered out the window to look at the victim. Let's call the bird "Ralph," for no specific reason. To my great surprise, Ralph was not dead. He was hunkered down, staring straight ahead. Other than his tiny chest heaving in and out, there was no other movement.

*Well, he'll soon be dead.* I imagined I'd be giving him a brief but respectable send-off into bird eternity.

Then I noticed dozens of other robins playfully diving from branch to branch, singing and darting through the crisp morning air. My front yard was like a playground full of first graders at recess. This wild, beautiful artistry had been unfolding in the background of my study time, but now my attention was thoroughly arrested.

As the erratic, syncopated dance around him continued, Ralph stared. Likely dying. Certain he would never fly again. Waiting for the end to come.

After a few moments, his friends began interacting with him—or so it appeared. Two or three at a time, the robins would dive into the yard, land in the grass near the sidewalk, bounce a little, tweet some, and then fly away quickly. It appeared they were communicating.

*Are they making fun of him or cheering him on?* If it were my brothers, the squawking would have been jeering: *Hey, everybody, did you see that? He hit the window! Lol!* They would have posted a video of it.

Either way, Ralph was utterly unresponsive. Sitting. Staring. Still breathing.

A full twenty minutes passed. I was mesmerized.

Almost imperceptibly, Ralph made the slightest of movements. He hopped about half an inch. No wings. No risk.

Several more moments passed as the cacophony and choreography of his fellow robins continued.

Then, there it was. Ralph hopped again.

Afraid to fly.

Alive but flummoxed.

Who wouldn't be? Imagine flying through the open sky and suddenly hitting a transparent barrier that knocked all reason out of you.

My guess was that Ralph was planning to play it safe for the rest of his life—*flying is for the . . .* Well, that doesn't work here.

Why couldn't I look away? More strangely, why had I left the tiny feather he deposited on my breakfast nook window?

Well, because I'm a lot like Ralph. I've been there. Soaring forward in ministry, imagining nothing but hopeful, clear skies, and then WHAM! The next thing I know, I wake up on a sidewalk, wondering where the sky went.

How many ministry walls have I hit? I stopped counting. How many invisible barriers have knocked me dizzy and left me afraid to do what I was called to do? Some walls are spiritual, others emotional or relational, and others are physical or material.

As a pastor or ministry leader, do you ever feel like Ralph?

Me too.

*Soaring* is for the gifted. Super-pastors. The risk-takers and the courageous. The leaders with great vision. But people like me fly into windows and stuff. We are sometimes dazed and fearful of soaring into our calling once again.

We have a hard time thinking about five-year plans and world-changing objectives (not that those aren't helpful—they are). Still, most days of pastoring are primarily about being faithful in today's needs while preparing for tomorrow's challenges. Usually, *today* is overwhelming enough. Jesus knew it would be like this—"Therefore do not be anxious about tomorrow, for tomorrow will be anxious for itself. Sufficient for the day is its own trouble" (Matt. 6:34).

Yeah, getting through today is a magnificent goal, especially after you've just kissed a window at thirty miles per hour.

### Sit. Stare. Breathe.

Maybe you are new to spiritual leadership and discovering the uniquely disheartening, breath-stealing aspects of ministry. Or perhaps this book comes to you later in the journey, after you've stuck a few feathers to nearby windows. Perhaps you feel as if you are done.

You may want to sit, stare, and hope to keep breathing. Me too, sometimes.

It's in these times that we start to wonder, *Am I the right person for this? Maybe I heard God wrong or misread the call signs. Hopping into some other vocation seems like a good solution.* You start to imagine a quiet, clock-in-clock-out career that doesn't include "the salvation of the world" in its job description or "blameless" in the list of qualifications.

Perhaps you're thinking, *I can't go on.*

Whatever your level of dismay—I'm honored that you opened this book.

Though I will often refer to the role of a pastor in the pages ahead, it's important to know that the experiences and solutions we will discover together are universal in their application. Anyone faithfully serving in gospel ministry will identify with and be strengthened in the chapters ahead.

> ANYONE FAITHFULLY SERVING IN GOSPEL MINISTRY WILL IDENTIFY WITH AND BE STRENGTHENED IN THE CHAPTERS AHEAD.

For all of ministry's unique challenges, I *love* being a spiritual leader. I'm early in my fourth decade in pastoral ministry and my second decade as senior pastor in a revitalizing church in New England. I'm writing from health, but only after traveling through many seasons of unhealth. Wellness is a fragile dynamic in a vocation of endless spiritual battle. It's not easy to come by or sustain, but it is possible and worth the journey.

Your wellness in Jesus is vital for God's people and for the gospel's sake.

This book is *not* a mutual moping manifesto. I avoid the "poor me" syndrome and the "it's so hard to be a pastor" thought stream. Sure it is. But every vocation has unique challenges as well as unique joys. Complaining doesn't resolve any real issues, and moping bypasses maturity and misses all the benefits of our call. In fact, grumbling is often a passive grab for sympathy, and "feel sorry for me" is a bad motivational tactic for any leader. (That's coming from a pretty good moper.)

So, with a bit of empathy and a lot of optimism, let's take an upward, more objective look at the flourishing soul and abundant life that Jesus promised (John 10:10). Let's discover the easy yoke and restful soul He offered in Matthew 11:28–30. Let's particularly pursue these in view of unique ministry stresses.

This book is best read from the sidewalk. It is not a book about becoming the exceptional super-pastor of a megachurch. This is not an instruction manual for "getting to the next level," "building something great for God," or "breaking-barriers numerical growth."

When you're counting broken bones, the idea of breaking an inflight speed record is almost insulting.

That said, you may be surprised how soul wellness—a healthy pastor and healthy church culture—is conducive to growth of many kinds. But that's secondary to the primary work Jesus desires to do in and through us. The goal is health in Jesus—which is energizing and life-giving. The byproduct is growth.

The Good Shepherd tends His sheep to health. He leads them to still waters and green pastures (Ps. 23), and He calls under-shepherds to lead His sheep *to* health *from* health.

*Wellness reproduces wellness.*

But how do Jesus' ideals reconcile with our reality—like flying into windows?

I'm there. I woke up this morning planning to write and ended up sitting, staring, and breathing for a while. I'm not even sure *why*. Spiritual battle can be that elusive—as transparent and invisible as a picture window is to a robin.

We are the weak ones. We wake up every day feeling like the wrong one for the job and wonder how long it will take people to figure out how "not together" we have it. It seems that for the pastorate, we are abnormally "normal."

We may not be confident and self-assured, but we love Jesus, love the gospel, and love helping people discover a grace relationship with the greatest Savior. It's just that sometimes we wake up on the sidewalk wondering if we're dead yet.

## Why This Book?

It's a crazy experience to be flying into safe, open skies, blissfully cruising—no, *soaring*, just as promised in Isaiah 40, right?—but then you slam into a wall, concussed into confusion.

Bible college, seminary, and early ministry dreams sent you flying with abandon and an almost narcotic surrender. You gave your whole heart and passion. You were confident your ministry flight would be *even better* than you imagined. "No eye has seen, nor ear heard, nor the heart of man imagined . . ." Isn't that the idea of 1 Corinthians 2:9?

*WHAM!* How did those ideals evaporate with such suddenness?

14

Sometimes we wonder, *Where did this wall come from? And why did God allow it to be there? Isn't He supposed to be "establishing our steps"* (Ps. 37:23), *"lighting our path"* (Ps. 119:105), *"making crooked places straight" and "going before" us* (Isa. 45:2), *and "make straight our paths"* (Prov. 3:6)? *Where did He go?* And why do we suddenly feel hesitant to try and uncertain that we have the strength to lead God's good people?

The sidewalk is a sad place with a skewed view of the world. From down here, it appears that all the other pastors are cruising beautifully. After all, social media reminds you that *everybody's* life is better than yours.

Do you ever feel hesitant to fly forward?

Me too.

But here's the good news: that's a feeling. Feelings can change when we expose them to truth. Hope can live again. We can love pastoring because God's strength is always renewable.

I pray these pages will provide some renewal for you—a recalibration toward wellness aiming at a steady, fruitful, and profoundly satisfying life as Jesus' servant.

---

So—back to Ralph.

Do you know what happened? He hopped a few more times and sat a little while, and his friends continued their dive patterns. After thirty minutes of reorientation and ten minutes of tentative hopping, Ralph found the edge of the sidewalk and leaped into the grass. He didn't cover much ground. Ten minutes resulted in ten inches.

But the following five minutes resulted in fifteen feet as Ralph's confidence revived. I couldn't help but cheer him on. *C'mon, man, fly! You can't hop forever. Give it another shot!* You can tell I was emotionally invested by this point. I hoped against hope that Ralph would resume doing what he was *created* to do. Imagine having wings but being afraid to use them.

Imagine having a *call* and giving up on it too soon.

Ralph didn't give up. I can't explain his avian logic, but without warning, he suddenly launched into the air and soared away. In one fear-defying split second, he returned to the sky—to his true nature—and I'm pretty sure I heard his friends celebrating.

I have not heard from Ralph since, so I imagine he is doing well. But how about you?

You may be dazed, but you were designed to soar on strong wings of grace. While you may need to catch your breath and reframe your heart—there can be wellness and sustained strength in your future. You *can* pastor from fullness.

There is a strong, steady approach to this tumultuous vocation.

Each word of this text is accompanied by a prayer for you that our time together will help you regain equilibrium. Our calling is always challenging, often confusing, but also wonderfully rewarding.

## Our Journey Together

**I write from my weak seasons.** My journey has often seemed like limping forward in a race where everyone else seems to be running. That's not self-cynicism or false humility. It's my genuine sense of it. If you track my social media, I glorify God there, not my struggles. Nevertheless, I am proficient in being weak. Thankfully, in God's economy, weakness is an advantage.

**I want to motivate you to develop your wellness plan.** I don't presume to impose my formula on you. There are no fast fixes for *your* renewed strength. You and your family are unique and have been given a unique calling and context. Your plan will not look like mine or someone else's. The journey before us will involve the courageous, principled discovery of what sustainable flourishing looks like in *your* context.

**This is about your journey and your wellness, not mine.** I may have faced similar challenges, and I hope to provide navigational resources and valuable practices. But our focus is for *you* to be joyfully airborne in service and to help you and those you love to abound in God's grace. Please allow my stories to glorify Jesus, not me. He's the real hero of our stories, and His grace is the true source of our strength.

**This book is not aimed at vetting a call that is legitimately doubted.** Unwellness can cause us to wrestle emotionally with *artificial* doubts. These doubts result from seasonal fatigue, spiritual resistance, or a sense of insufficiency. They do not substantively indicate that one is in the wrong vocation. Vetting a call is an excellent thing to do. Not everybody is called to this. But I am writing to those who *know* they are called despite the difficulties.

**This book is not designed to "sell you" on gospel ministry.** Suppose you are legitimately considering another vocation. In that case, this book may help you vet those considerations, but I'm writing on the assumption that you are *in* and intend to *stay in*, but that you hope for a different kind of "in." Stepping away from the ministry is sometimes God's will for various reasons, but arriving at that conclusion is beyond the scope of these pages.

**Our journey in these pages is composed of three parts.** Part One is *Cultivate a Strong Core*. We will retool our unseen motives and unspoken expectations, uncover how we sabotage ourselves, and seek to strengthen the inner man.

In Part Two—*Nurture a Flourishing Soul*—we'll explore personal disciplines or customs that maintain wellness and renew strength on multiple levels. This section will involve more than temporary solutions or quick fixes. These pivotal conversations will aim at long-term sustainability. Try not to rush or shortcut through this section.

Part Three is *Lead a Healthy Culture*, where we'll explore how a gospel-shaped culture renews strength. This will give us some resistance to predictable toxins that create unhealthy conditions.

Part One is your heart. Part Two is your personal life. Part Three is your ministry environment. The three work together *inseparably* to sustainably renew strength. If any of these three dynamics collapse or become toxic, the other two will rapidly decline as well.

We aim for a *reset* and a new life trajectory. We are targeting a complete, biblical recalibration. The values and practices we will explore are not short-term sedatives to keep you in the race, but rather a long-term approach to joyful and fruitful durability.

Together we will discover a new pace, a new resilience, and a new kind of sustainability to face the unique pressures and challenges of twenty-first-century spiritual leadership.

Does the idea of *wellness*—emotional, spiritual, mental, relational, physical, and material health—seem incompatible with your current role? Does it seem unattainable at your present pace? Has serving *from health* become an elusive concept, and you're tired of living on the ragged edge, hanging by a thread, feeling like a noble but miserable martyr?

I get it.

*There is another way.*

You can thrive again. A heavy dose of reality may have whacked your dreams, but Jesus can recover them, rewrite them, and ultimately lead you to deep fulfillment in His beautiful story.

Brokenness is always God's prerequisite for blessedness. He doesn't leave brokenness broken.

———

Welcome to the sidewalk, my dazed friend.

God does deep work here. He meets us in the bruising. Then in His merciful way, He slowly and safely lifts us back into flight for His purposes.

Since we're both sitting here for a while, catching our breath, how about we chat? Let me share some things God has taught me on the sidewalks.

I'm confident that God desires to reorient you toward the healthy calling you crave but perhaps stopped believing *can be.*

God is not dead. Neither are you. You lost a few feathers, and you're rattled.

Rest up. Retool. Recalibrate.

Recover the dream.

Soon enough, you'll be riding the wind!

# Part One

# CULTIVATE A STRONG CORE

## 5 Decisions That Grow Deep Strength

*I love you, O LORD, my strength. Psalm 18:1*

God's strength comes to us in counterintuitive ways. He fortifies us through weakness, delivers us through disruptions, and infuses courage by calling us to intimidating assignments.

Why? Because our hearts gravitate to human strength—visible, measurable, tangible forms of power and success. We prefer strategies and tactics over waiting and depending. But His strength transcends our best plans and infuses our deepest fears. His truth anchors us at our core.

The starting point of steady strength is a strong gospel core—the motivational and aspirational center of our service to Jesus.

As we begin our journey, we will examine five decisions of a durable core.

*#1—Embrace Insufficiency*
*#2—Seek Jesus*
*#3—Delight in Obedience*
*#4—Celebrate Gospel Durability*
*#5—Grow a Gospel Identity*

*Thy God hath commanded thy strength: strengthen, O God, that which thou hast wrought for us. Psalm 68:28 KJV*

## CHAPTER ONE

# THE WRONG ONE FOR THE JOB

## EMBRACE INSUFFICIENCY

*But he said to me, "My grace is sufficient for you, for my power is made perfect in weakness." Therefore I will boast all the more gladly of my weaknesses, so that the power of Christ may rest upon me. For the sake of Christ, then, I am content with weaknesses. . . . For when I am weak, then I am strong.*

2 Corinthians 12:9–10

It was pitch black. I was wide awake in bed at 2 a.m., staring at the ceiling. My wife, Dana, slept peacefully beside me, but there was no peace for me. Just turmoil. Nearly twelve years later, I'm still unsure if that scene was wrestling, negotiating, or rebelling. God and I were having an ongoing conversation, but I was not being cooperative.

Fear dominated my mind, and relevant excuses were abundant. I was trying to convince God that He was in error (absurd—yes, I know), that He shouldn't call me to a senior pastorate, and that I was the wrong guy for the job. I was looking for any excuse to give me an out.

Admittedly, there is nothing wrong with aspiring to be a senior pastor (1 Tim. 3:1), but it wasn't something *I* desired. First, I didn't believe I had the senior leader gift mix. Second, I had never sensed that particular call. Third, I was sure of my fit as a "support man" (sort of like Joshua to Moses . . . gulp!). Fourth, I was comfortable with my present assignment, although God was making it increasingly *un*comfortable. And finally, seeing the unhappiness, grumpiness, and misery of some pastors, I didn't want the burden.

I feared losing the joy of ministry.

This negotiation between me and God had lasted several months. He was pursuing my heart, and His Word was specifically convicting. Circumstances were relentlessly validating. His Spirit was ceaselessly confirming. But my fear, self-cynicism, and risk aversion were ultimately winning.

That night was the final round of wrestling. For weeks I hadn't slept much and didn't have an appetite. My wife patiently and silently watched me struggle, giving God space to do His work within me.

As I lay there, I realized He was changing the conversation. Scripture had moved from calling to correcting to warning. It's important to say I never had the overt intention of disobeying God. But I was hoping I could wear Him down, change His mind, or talk Him out of it—like a teen-parent argument.

But that night He seemed to draw a line in the sand, as if to say, *Stop. It's now or never. I'm not negotiating. I've been patient, but now it's time to obey or disobey. I will either deal with you as an obedient child or a disobedient one. Which will it be?*

In the silence, facing that gauntlet of a question, I held my breath, then answered. "Lord, I will obey. I repent of fear and argumentativeness. I surrender. I'll go wherever. I'll do whatever. Would You consider three requests? Would You help me sensitively navigate my resignation and communication? Second, could You spare me from looking for a church? Point me expressly to the church where You are leading. And third, this will be unimaginably complex and painful. Would You assure me that You are going with us?" (See Ex. 33:14–15; Josh. 1:9; Matt. 28:20; Acts 18:10; and 1 Thess. 5:24 for similar prayers or promises.)

My last, fleeting request was, "Lord—if You would provide a building, I will preach the gospel and pray that You will fill it with new believers." As a peaceful night's sleep finally began, I remember drifting off, thinking: *What did I get myself into?*

It was the first night I had fallen deeply asleep in months. My next memory was waking refreshed. For the first time in many days, I was energized by God's pervasive peace. Crazy how surrendering to God's vast unknown can be so comforting.

My wife noticed the change with intrigue. I explained that the fight was over, and I had lost. In truth, it was a *win*, for true surrender is always a spiritual victory. It's a good thing when God vanquishes our hearts. My struggle with God was over, and we would follow Him—though we didn't know where, when, or how.

Having observed my prolonged ordeal and having already surrendered personally, Dana responded with remarkable optimism and faith. While she didn't desire to be anywhere else in ministry and wasn't looking forward to the significant losses we would experience, she had sensed God's unfolding work and yielded to Him much sooner than I did.

She assured me of her heart. This would be a *together* adventure, and I was thankful to have a faith-filled wife. We had a deeply shared sense of call and were simultaneously nervous and excited. Something supernatural and wonderful was unfolding in our lives, but it was leading us into deep waters in unfamiliar territory. While choosing to obey God brought peace, it also opened a new world of possibilities for fear and worry.

Suddenly, our future was a terrifyingly blank slate.

But God writes amazing stories when we give Him blank slates.

## A Call to Insufficiency

How often have you thought, *I'm the wrong guy for this*?

Right. And wrong. At the same time.

Deep pastoral wellness begins with *reckoning*—a reality check of sorts. Please don't let these following few chapters seem negative in tone. Instead, see them as diagnostic. Without complaining, we need an objective view of ministry realities. Gospel service consumes our souls in ways that God counters with offsetting graces.

Let's ask God to open our eyes to things we would rather deny, ignore, or escape. Let's own the truth of this deep end of the ocean in which we swim. Yes, we are in over our heads and treading water. Yes, we are the right "wrong guys" for the job. Yes, we are inadequate.

A call to pastor is a call to *insufficiency*.

Ironic. God calls us to things we are not "up for." He sends us into impossibility. He delights in exploiting our weaknesses. Sometimes He even tells us, *It's not going to work!*

He told Moses to go to Pharaoh but predicted that Pharaoh wouldn't listen. He sent Ezekiel to Hebrew exiles but preemptively said they would not hear. He commanded Jeremiah not to be afraid of people's faces. He prepared Paul to be arrested in Jerusalem. He exhorted John the Baptist not to be offended in Him. In each of these cases and others, God called insufficient people to substantial tasks and prepared them to be let down in the process. Step one—"Follow Me." Step two—"Be let down."

Death always precedes resurrection.

This is interesting when juxtaposed against the modern ministry narrative, which is something like: Step one—"Follow Me," and step two—"Everything turns out great!"

Christian motivational speech teaches us to aim high, be winners, and get the job done. But in spiritual leadership, the first criterion is "Be weak." Perhaps you knew from the start that you were insufficient.

Or maybe you knew it theologically but secretly believed you would crush it. After all, some aim at immediate celebrity, confident they will quickly rise to it.

On the other hand, perhaps insufficiency is self-evident, having knocked you flat to the ground in stunned dismay. The *experience* of insufficiency is unnerving and overwhelming. The moment our inadequacy hits us like a wall (and it will), it's enough to make us want to walk away or render us unhealthy until we do.

We all want to be good at what we do. Who doesn't desire to succeed? We dream of being useful to God. This is healthy from a biblical perspective, but it is also counter to the breaking, humiliating realization that God's work is drastically bigger than we are.

Insufficiency is built into gospel ministry, and our weakness is not a surprise to God; it's one of His unique qualifiers. But the *experience* of it is dismaying. Our daily acquaintance with insufficiency can grow wearisome.

Insufficiency is permanent. Remaining in ministry means we never rid ourselves of this unwelcome companion. No amount of experience, education, time, or supposed success can quash this ever-present pest. We will know weakness like nothing we've ever known.

The *normal* pastoral call is perpetually reacquainted with the constant, often condemning voice of insufficiency. Sounds like everyone's career dreams, right?

In my imagination, that voice is the annoying kid in the movie *The Polar Express*.[1] I can hear him daily: *You will never be a good pastor. Give up while you still can. You're such a disappointment!*

## The Paradoxical First Step to Wellness

In ministry, you're going to wake up every day facing needs, expectations, and spiritual challenges that are far beyond your reach and ability. These things laugh at talent, spit on education, trample experience, and trump every imaginable preparatory strategy. We swim in stormy, deep waters, and they are constantly changing.

You will never *feel* like the right guy for the job. You will never *feel* like you've got this in hand. You will never *feel* up to it or sufficient for the needs of God's people.

Every day you will coexist with insufficiency. You will live with a limp, yet you are called to run your race with patience (Heb. 12:1–2). You will be confronted with strong feelings of finiteness and walk through life with a general low-grade sense of inadequacy.

This is God's intention and design.

Why?

> *Insufficiency requires us to depend upon*
> *and point others to a sufficient Savior.*

Think about it. If we believed we were sufficient, what a disaster it would create! Our ego would project a contrived image, and we would find it impossible to be the saviors we pretend to be. We would exhaust ourselves attempting to live up to our phony images, and eventually, we would become the object of scorn from the people we let down.

Trying to come off as sufficient is nothing but fakery looking for a way to fall apart.

We aren't sufficient. Jesus is sufficient. God's people need *Him*, not *us*. They need us like the Israelites needed John the Baptist—we *point* to Him.

Insufficiency is built into the faith-life.

How does this relate to a "wellness plan"? It's a paradox, like many things in Scripture. Most wellness talk attempts to teach us to deny or defeat negative ideas. Most formulas prescribe self-help and self-esteem books and coach us to overcome with positivity. Psychobabble says, *Look in the mirror and say, "You've got this," and then go out and build a great church and change the world!*

God's Word essentially says, *Repeat after me—"I don't got this. But Jesus has got me, and He's got this!"* (Grammar intentionally butchered for emphasis.)

Pastoral wellness begins with embracing insufficiency as the ever-present reminder that we are not "the Savior." Acknowledging insufficiency delivers us from the burden of being the hero of the story.

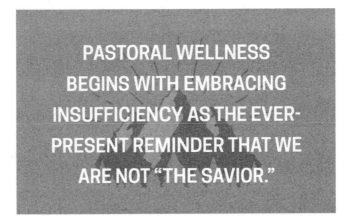

PASTORAL WELLNESS BEGINS WITH EMBRACING INSUFFICIENCY AS THE EVER-PRESENT REMINDER THAT WE ARE NOT "THE SAVIOR."

Now, *embracing it* does not mean giving in or giving up. It does not mean that despair owns the narrative in your head. It certainly does not mean walking away. *Embrace it* means reckoning with reality, accepting this new, pesky forever friend, and expecting God to leverage it into His strength.

The truth is that Jesus does not expect us to be sufficient. Teaching this to ourselves and others helps everyone remember that *you* are not the Savior, Jesus is. He must increase; we must decrease (John 3:30). Decreasing is healthy. It is safe and true. It is a Christlike descent into wellness. We lower ourselves into spiritual and emotional health. We downsize our view of self. It is the only way to sustain a healthy servant-hearted trajectory, and I believe it is the first step in developing a strong core for a steady journey in spiritual leadership.

## The Good News of Insufficiency

Embracing insufficiency is not self-deprecation or denial of ability, talent, giftedness, education, preparation, or all other good resources for ministry. It is an objective reckoning with the reality of a gap.

There is a great gulf between the totality of *me* and the totality of the spiritual needs of those I love and serve. The corrective realization is that there is *no gulf* between the fullness of Jesus and the magnitude of those needs. Jesus fills the gap.

The infinitude of our assignment—meeting the spiritual needs of people—viewed against the severity of our insufficiency and weakness will create one of two responses: self-centered despondency or Jesus-centered dependence. Self-cynicism simply thinks *I can't do this.* But reliant faith experiences a resolved sort of liberation, believing *God will do this.*

The faith view of weakness is optimistic. Our awareness of insufficiency can either level us or liberate us. If we take it to the wrong place emotionally and psychologically, we will walk away and find a vocation we can handle. Therefore, insufficiency must be processed biblically.

Insufficiency isn't something we overcome or defeat. It's something that compels us to release ourselves into Jesus' sufficiency. His strength makes us free from the soul-crushing burden of trying to do what only He can. This is the first step to being an authentic, visible example of the gospel life—one in which we stop depending on what we can do and begin depending on what Jesus has done.

God's people do not need to see a sufficient leader. They need to see an insufficient leader joyfully trusting and obeying a sufficient Savior.

This is what it means to *live out* the gospel so that God's people hear it in our teaching *and* see it in our living. We declare it and display it. And they see it not only in a moral lifestyle but more abundantly and clearly in a weak but trusting faith walk. They see us growing up in the gospel—as they are. They know that we run and limp simultaneously, which is okay because Jesus has already run and won our race.

## A Funeral for Sufficiency

I imagine we should schedule a funeral for sufficiency. Mourn its nonexistence. Grieve its absence. But only for a moment. Play a short dirge. Shed a tear or two. Bid it farewell with finality. But then see it for the iron taskmaster that it was.

Pretending to be sufficient would have imprisoned you to a life behind a curtain, like the Wizard of Oz. You would be a flaming, oversized bluster in image only—fearsome and apparently powerful, but actually a desperate little man, hiding in fear of exposure.

Contrived sufficiency is the prelude to catastrophic collapse.

The gospel says, "Who you truly are is enough in Jesus." Open the curtain. Let down the smokescreen. Unveil the insecurities and release the pretense. Jesus likes the little guy behind the curtain, or in a tree (Luke 19), or on a night-shrouded lake (John 21), or crouching by a winepress (Judg. 6). He loves to release us from our exhausting masquerades. He sets us free to be weak followers of a strong Savior.

Doesn't the gospel begin with insufficiency? Doesn't our relationship with God begin with, "God, be merciful to me, a sinner" (Luke 18:13)? As with salvation, the only way we can be useful for His purposes is to be insufficient. We aren't just "weak." We feel it, live with it, and fight with it every day as it presses uninvited back into our psyches.

Embracing it means we appropriate it to its rightful place—a *reality* but not a *limitation*. In God's economy, weakness is the first qualification of the call.

Do you know what's kind of sad about the Wizard of Oz? The man behind the curtain was so likable. How long he hid in fear, grasping for power, when he could have joyfully, restfully played himself, a wise, gentle benefactor to Oz. I'm certain the lollipop kids would have preferred his gentle self to the fiery, oversized image he had constructed.

Guess what? Your church family would too. No one really expects you to be sufficient unless you convince them otherwise. If you try to, some will believe you, exponentially increasing your performance troubles. A better path is to regularly admit to yourself and others your insufficiency—not in self-deprecation, but in honest, Christ-dependence. This will keep all eyes on Jesus as Savior, not you.

Let Jesus release you from the crushing burden of sufficiency. Equally, refuse to allow insufficiency to dominate your heart's narrative. A healthy pastor shakes hands with insufficiency daily but then tells it to take a seat before the sufficient Savior—Jesus.

Embrace insufficiency. It's a pain, but in its annoying way, it also makes you free.

You don't have to be a savior. Jesus already is.

## CHAPTER TWO

# A GROWING FOLLOWER

## SEEK JESUS

*Therefore be imitators of God, as beloved children.
And walk in love, as Christ loved us . . .*

EPHESIANS 5:1–2

I was sitting in a room full of next-generation pastors hoping to encourage them. Though the opportunity was a privilege, the pre-teaching anxiety overshadowed that fact. My friend Kurt, tasked with introducing me, stood to speak in the crowded room. I wasn't looking forward to the introduction because it is almost always an uncomfortable moment for a speaker.

When I stand to teach God's Word, I'm a fellow struggler. Flowery introductions are awkward and leave me feeling like I need to correct the record. But imagine my surprise when Kurt said, "I asked Cary's son Lance, 'How should I introduce your dad?'" Lance, a fellow pastor, had traveled with me to the event and knows me all too well.

My mind raced. *This is going to get ugly. Lance has a few too many stories in his arsenal.* But then another thought came: *I guess embarrassing is better than flowery.* Knowing my son as honest but also gracious, I was intrigued.

Kurt continued. "Here's what Lance said, 'My dad is a growing Christian.'"

My sense of relief and gratitude was palpable. My soul celebrated for a second. I don't remember what Kurt said next because I was overcome with joy over how my oldest son encapsulated his perception of his dad.

It was an honest, unvarnished assessment of a regular guy trying to follow Jesus faithfully and encourage others to do the same. Lance's viewpoint helped uncomplicate my call. It wasn't over the top, performance-oriented, or achievement-focused. It wasn't artificially inflated. "A growing Christian." Yes, that's it.

*I can be that, and I can be that for the rest of my life.*

## The Simple Role of Pastoring

Put me on the witness stand to testify to "what I am," and this is my answer: I'm a follower of Jesus. I love and trust Him. His love is so lavish and wonderful that I want to help others know it, experience it, and live out of it. Along the way, I want to keep growing in Him. Growing is slow, steady, and sometimes painful work, but thankfully I have the rest of my life. The hard work is His, and He never gets tired of me or gives up on me (Phil. 1:6). It's all unfolding at His pace. Every time I try to be something more, I wake up dazed on the sidewalk, asking myself what I'm trying to prove. Soon enough Jesus reminds me *He* is enough and growing in Him is my primary calling.

The word "pastor" or the title of a senior leader can often elicit strange and quirky assumptions in people's minds. When people find out I'm a pastor, they often grow uncomfortable. From the first mention of the title, the conversation changes with unspoken and un-clear dynamics. It's not uncommon for guests to introduce themselves by saying, "We've been afraid to meet you." Insert my facepalm here.

Titles or positions can build up strange ideas in our own heads as well. Leaders feel the weight of the expectations of others and the pres-sure to understand and even exceed those expectations. We can live under the burden of having to be at our best 100 percent of the time.

The obvious conclusion of this thought flow is: *They don't want me—they want Jesus! And I'm not Him.*

While spiritual leaders wear many hats, let's talk about *essence*. What is the role of a pastor, most essentially? What perspective brings the role in line with the heart of Jesus? What if we could reduce spiritual leadership to its essence and return to that again and again?

For the sake of our sanity, let's simplify.

Pastoring God's people is not about "becoming a great leader." Plenty of leaders overemphasize the idea of "human greatness." Often the explicit or implicit messaging is this, *Do great things and become great like other great men.* (As a side note, Dana has a recurring nickname for me—O Great One. She laughs hysterically every time she says it.)

The Bible does refer to great men, cities, battles, and work—things grand in scope—but our modern culture and too often our ministry vernacular make greatness an identity to pursue, which is dangerous.

Though Jesus called our works "great," we have no mandate from Him to personally "become great." This pursuit is an empty ego trip that will eventually break us. Forget about personal greatness. Let's focus on something that honors God and our calling, and that is within our reach.

Many excellent volumes have been written about the theological nature and operational function of a pastor or spiritual leader. We could deep dive into Paul's letters to Timothy and Titus, and Peter's letters as well. We could exhaustively examine the concept of pastoring, and we should, as a life journey. But for brevity and focus, let's keep it simple.

The root word for pastor is "shepherd" in both the Old and New Testaments (Eph. 4:11; Jer. 3:15). We know that God's church has one shepherd, the chief Shepherd, Jesus. But Peter teaches us to "feed the flock of God which is among you" (1 Peter 5:2 KJV). This feeding is to be delivered in a way that gives willing, loving, sincere, and eager oversight—caring for and leading—without becoming authoritarian or domineering over God's sheep (vv. 2–4). God's people are *His* possession, not ours.

This kind of leadership is neither at the top, bottom, nor middle of the organizational flow chart. It doesn't chart well. "Under-shepherd" works, but it's an awkward term. We shepherd sheep, and we *are* sheep simultaneously. We are sheep who assistant-shepherd other sheep, and one of our primary functions is feeding. This is to teach, oversee, and provide soul care for spiritual health.

Imagine healthy sheep growing well in a good pasture under a good shepherd's faithful care. Think of the quality of life of those sheep—safety, calm, provision, restfulness, peace, wholeness. *Shalom.*

Every human heart craves this shalom life, and its absence is the root of all anxiety, fear, rage, and despair. Shalom is both spiritual and material—we experience it *personally* in Christ and then corporately in *community*. This rare reality is Jesus' wonderful, ultimate destination for His sheep, but we can't lead others into it if we don't experience it ourselves.

All of this thinking begs one vital question:

**How does Jesus shepherd?**

On the one hand, we have four gospels and a New Testament filled with the gentle-natured compassion of Jesus toward His fearful and sometimes fickle followers. On the other hand, we have an expansive Old Testament revealing God's lavish and loving heart toward His believing flock.

But perhaps the greatest shepherding profile is Psalm 23. Jesus leads His sheep to still waters and green pastures, the sort of environment where sheep thrive in health, multiply in fruitfulness, and rest in comforting provision. Imagine the privilege of being a conduit—a distributor or a facilitator of this shalom life—abundant life flowing from Jesus to His sheep. Relish the idea that Jesus would extend to us the profound and beautiful opportunity to help His sheep experience His love, presence, and gentle care. Dream of cultivating His people in a still waters, green pasture kind of church, and dream of experiencing that personally as well.

Jesus makes this dream possible in us—to shepherd and lead His sheep into a church culture and spiritual environment that resembles still waters and green pastures. This is *my* goal—shepherdly-ness, not greatness. The first expends itself for others' wellness; the second exploits others for personal gain. True shepherds refuse to exploit the sheep and instead choose to expend themselves in love.

This is one reason Lance's observation was so meaningful. I know how Jesus has shepherded me for the last five decades. He is patient and faithful. He ever graces my soul with infinite love. He truly is the Good Shepherd.

For this reason, keeping it simple helps me to continue forward: I'm a growing, loving follower of Jesus, helping other people love and follow Jesus with me. As an assistant shepherd, I believe my care should look ever more like His, working with Him for His flock's blessing and health (1 Cor. 3:9).

If only books and classes made it this simple. We think, *If only it were this simple.*

It is.

Ministry leadership becomes complicated when we take on His responsibilities and lose sight of ours. Our roles grow murky and overwhelming when we believe the endless, internal suppositions that the problems are ours to solve—from broken toilets to broken marriages. Pastors encounter many broken things each day, and we always will. Yet, a greater Shepherd is cultivating, redeeming, and renewing those broken things.

I am not the great Redeemer of broken things. He is. I don't have to fix every mess or right every wrong. He will. The essence of our call is far simpler than the complexity we face. It is to love Him first. Love them well. And lead others to experience His love.

Period.

I can't be the great Shepherd, but I can lead others to Him. I can't remake, reshape, or transform hearts. But He does.

With this simple perspective, immense pastoral pressures are removed—falling from our shoulders to His. The ensuing relief that emerges always brings a fresh, energizing delight in the privilege of spiritual leadership—under-shepherding in the shadow of the Good Shepherd.

How cool!

## It's All about Loving Jesus

In John 21, Jesus didn't call for Peter to do penance for his failures. He didn't command him to be great or build great things. He didn't issue sweeping challenges for Peter to execute grand designs. He asked one simple question three times—*Do you love Me?* (John 21:15–17). *Think about it. Do you love Me? Yes, you are flawed. Yes, you are insufficient.*

*But . . . Do. You. Love. Me?*

Three times, following Peter's tentative and insecure responses, Jesus gave the same simple directive:

*Feed my lambs. Tend my sheep. Feed my sheep.*

Jesus used two operative verbs. The first and third mean "feed and keep feeding." Essentially, *This is the new you, Peter, and your new life assignment*. The middle verb is the same word Peter later used that means "to shepherd or tend" continually (1 Peter 5).

In essence, *If you love me, then feed and care for those I love as I would.*

So let's bring it home to you and me right now.

Set aside our understood weakness and insufficiency. Move past our previously errant motives or core expectations. Right here, right now, is Jesus asking, *Do you love me?*

Does Jesus call you to feed, care for, and love His sheep as He does? Then love Him and love them. Lead them into the still waters and green pastures of His Word and His church. Devote yourself to a personal, healthy relationship with Jesus and then a healthy church environment where others can grow in grace.

Consider the inception of your service to Him. Why did you initially enter ministry? Probably because you loved Jesus and wanted others to have that same relationship. It was simple, wasn't it? The desire Jesus gave you was not complex in essence. So, where has that essence been lately?

Is it overwhelmed by a world gone mad with global crises and political pressures? Is it latent and sitting static at the bottom of a mile-long task list? Perhaps it is frustrated, unfulfilled, and nursing wounds from the people you tried to help who didn't want help, or maybe dismayed by those you thought were committed who suddenly ghosted you. Like many before you, maybe you're losing hope from not seeing visible evidence of your effectiveness.

For this moment, look past these momentary realities. Where is that original love for Jesus that simply desired to help others love and follow Him?

This is the essence of pastoring, the essence of all church health, and the essence of your soul health. Pastoral ministry is, at its God-formed core, the overflow of a heart well loved by Jesus. It is a genuine relationship with Jesus on display, overflowing into others, that they might choose to enter the same (John 7:38). Anything less is contrived and forced. Anything else makes ministry a job or a performance—just another day in the office, going through the motions, playing the part.

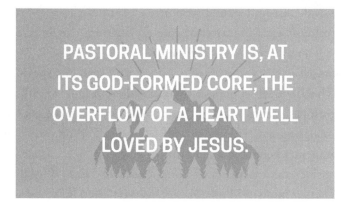

PASTORAL MINISTRY IS, AT ITS GOD-FORMED CORE, THE OVERFLOW OF A HEART WELL LOVED BY JESUS.

Maybe your ministry's beginning wasn't this pure or straightforward, but it should have been, and it can be now. Perhaps your motives were more socially shaped or externally pressed into you. Maybe gospel ministry was expected, imposed, inherited, or ingrained. You were likely compelled by a variety of motives—perhaps even a subconscious desire for affirmation, identity, or achievement.

Spiritual leaders can be plagued by dueling sets of internal desires. The pure desires seek to herald good news, sharing our stories and pointing people to Jesus, like Paul and others. But the toxic desires, sometimes lurking in the shadows, come from a flesh that desires affirmation and identity (3 John 9). I wrote about this at length in my book *Stop Trying: How to Receive—Not Achieve—Your Real Identity.*[1]

If your journey into gospel ministry involved anything more than simple, personal love for Jesus and longing to love others to Him, those motives must be purged. If ministry is about anything more than loving and leading people as Jesus would—denominationally, socially, culturally, personally—you will always be plagued by an agitated, unfulfilled heart.

Recently, my wife and I spent some time at a beautiful beach. I wear shoes pretty much everywhere I go, but this time she talked me into going barefoot.

"Your feet need to breathe," she said.

So, there I was with my breathing feet, and whack! A bed of pine needles I walked across was filled with burrs. Without warning, six of them punctured the soft soles of my typically Reebok-clad feet. The pain quickly overshadowed the spectacular beauty and my "breathing feet" because now they were bleeding! Hobbling my way to a sandy spot, I assessed the damage and began to remove the prickly annoyances, even as they reattached themselves to my fingertips. By the way, my feet have since learned to breathe *inside* my Reeboks.

Like those burrs, impure ministry motives will persistently puncture your heart, and the barbs are poisonous. These motives distract us from loving Jesus and prevent us from loving others well from a pure heart.

## Loving Jesus and Loving to Shepherd

The title "pastor" is far more an asset than a liability. We have the privilege of entering into the most profound and eternal work of Jesus in the human soul. Have you forgotten the simple delight of loving Jesus and loving others as He does?

Here's how Jesus reminded me of the joyful essence of gospel ministry.

I was sitting against the window on a connecting flight between Atlanta and Pensacola in March of 2020—two days before the world shut down for COVID. Before takeoff, a kind lady sat next to me. A few minutes into the flight, I asked what was taking her to Pensacola.

She responded that she was from Europe and was planning to visit family for a few days.

Then she returned the question, "What brings you to Pensacola?"

Immediately I was torn. My answer would most likely ostracize me and shut down the conversation. So, I chose to be vague.

"I'm teaching at a retreat for pastors and their wives." I left it with that simple statement.

Then, she slowly asked, "So . . . you . . . are . . . a pastor?"

*I knew it, she is uncomfortable.*

I answered with a wince in my heart, "Yes, I am . . ."

*She's probably going to move to another seat.*

The following pause left me hanging as this stranger visibly and audibly caught her breath, placing her hand on her heart. She appeared to hold back tears. Then she asked another hesitant question. "Could I talk to you?"

Delighted, I quickly responded, "Yes, of course. I *live* to talk to people!"

Her puzzling sigh and warm smile expressed relief. "I think you may be the answer to my prayers."

No one has ever said this to me except Dana. (Okay, that was a joke, but honestly . . .) The statement seemed over the top, but she continued to explain. She had grown up in a fiercely religious family and had become disillusioned with God and life, having recently faced a series of complex family trials. Her performance-based religion had failed her, and she was desperate for God.

She said, "Only last night I prayed, 'God if You are there, I need to know You. Please help me. Please give me the truth.'"

I smiled. "Actually, given those circumstances, I think I may be the answer to your prayers after all!" We both laughed.

For the next forty-five minutes, we contrasted the false salvation of "works" to the true salvation of the biblical Jesus—by grace through faith—an inexpressible gift of a loving God (2 Cor. 9:15). I have rarely, if ever, spoken to a person who was so one-step-ahead-of-me on every gospel point and so eager to receive God's saving grace. For example, as I described the oppression of works-based religions, she expressed deep frustration with a god who loves conditionally and cheaply.

She pleaded with me, "If God is so good, then why can't He love me without condition?"

The tears streamed as she finally saw the Jesus of Scripture for the first time. Just before our plane landed, she welcomed Jesus into her life as Savior and entered a grace-shaped relationship with Him rather than a transactional one. Her spiritual relief was palpable as we quietly celebrated. She was overjoyed to meet my Savior and to know His grace.

At that moment, the burdens and pressures of the ministry evaporated. Whatever I carried on that plane was immeasurably lighter in contrast to the profound joy of redeeming love. What a privilege to bear the label of *pastor*—someone she *wanted* and had prayed for a chance to talk to.

It's easy to lose perspective. It's easy to grow distant from our "first love" for our Lord (Rev. 2:4). But it's also easy to return to Him. "Remember therefore from where you have fallen; repent . . ." (v. 5). Renew your first love. Embrace Jesus afresh—as you did at first.

The love of Christ, when experienced personally, causes us to love Him in return and naturally produces a desire to love others into His love. This *first love* is the only pure, sustainable, viable motivation for Christian ministry. It energizes us with mature, gospel-shaped intentions. It is an ever-growing, evergreen kind of love that substantially provides steady strength in service.

Of its own virtue, this love organically overflows into grace-driven labor that desires to serve others with His heart. It is life-giving and energizing. In the seasons of waning strength, it is renewing.

Jesus calls us to this sustainable motivation—His love for us and our responsive love for Him. All other motivation is a withering experience slowly moving toward deprivation and burnout. Pastoring Jesus' sheep is primarily about loving and following Him personally and then letting Him care for and love His sheep through us.

A pastor is simply a growing follower of Jesus saying to other people, "Follow Jesus with me."

Wherever, whenever, and however that unfolds, it is always beautiful! The more we add to this simple idea, the more our hearts are misled, and our souls suffer.

Here's the awesome thing about loving Jesus. Even during the hard times, we know our future holds more unexpected gospel conversations like the one I had on the plane. His grace through us to others becomes an energizing stream. It leads us forward, not by success addiction, identity desires, or personal achievement, but by simple love. We anticipate His next work over our next accomplishment.

Can we love Him deeply to love others purely? At the depths of our being, personal wellness is a byproduct of what we love, what we hunger and thirst for, or what we chase after. If we pursue a particular version of success, we may or may not find it. If we yearn to love Jesus and love others well, we will succeed in the only ways that matter from eternity's perspective.

Can you say it with me?

"I'm a growing Christian. Jesus loves me, and I love Him back! Out of that grows all else."

*Do. You. Love. Me?*

"Yes, Lord. Imperfectly. But yes."

*Feed. My. Sheep.*

## CHAPTER THREE

# THE PARADOX OF SUCCESS

## DELIGHT IN OBEDIENCE

*"Let not the wise man boast in his wisdom, let not the mighty man boast in his might, let not the rich man boast in his riches, but let him who boasts boast in this, that he understands and knows me, that I am the LORD who practices steadfast love, justice, and righteousness."*

JEREMIAH 9:23–24

*What have I gotten into?* Those were my thoughts when God was disrupting my plan, but I imagine they were Ezekiel's thoughts as well. Let's visit the ancient Iraqi desert.

### An Epic, Unhappy Birthday

The ancient Hebrew version of "Happy Birthday" must have twisted itself into a dark, dissonant melody in Ezekiel's mind. His thirtieth birthday is spent unimaginably far from home. He is alone, sitting on the bank of an irrigation canal in the middle of the desert (modern-day Iraq). In the distance looms the pagan city of Babylon and, on the city's edge, a refugee camp of miserable Hebrew exiles. In every direction, blistering barrenness extends beyond the horizon. The dusty wind stirs up little comfort but plenty of eye irritation.

Ezekiel's mind vacillates between his present distress and his distant home. Perhaps he questions God. Or maybe he muses over Jeremiah's messages. No doubt, he tries to wrap his head around God's disruptive plan. Despite the apparent circumstances, somehow he is certain God is still good.

Even in exile, Ezekiel remains lovingly devoted to His Lord. God seems a million miles away from this place, along with the young man's hopes to become a priest at age thirty. In the mind of an ancient Israelite, God's presence rested in Jerusalem, not Babylon. *Temple Mount. The glorious City of God. Zion. The place of covenant sacrifice and festive celebration where Messiah has been promised to reign forever.* This is where Ezekiel's dreams would have landed him.

God would have seemed far from this miserable band of refugees in this distant desert. This scene appears to be nothing but a dirty canal and a lonely Hebrew saying goodbye to his twenties—wistfully remembering a home he will never see again. Adding insult to injury, his divine instructions are to seek the peace of the pagans (Jer. 29:7). Rather than serving the Most High God in His temple at Jerusalem, Ezekiel has a divine life sentence of banishment in Babylon. How confusing.

Let this sink in. Though Ezekiel was a devoted follower of God, preparing to be a priest—a shepherd in Israel—He could not see or feel God in his situation. Exile halted his graduation from seminary, shredded his life map, and thrust him into obscurity. He likely meditated on these complex realities while sitting by that river.

Little did he know how *close* God was.

What an unusual call when viewed through modern eyes. The church growth movement would have difficulty recommending

Ezekiel's ministry formula. In every way, his assignment was counterintuitive. Ours can be too, and we can learn from Ezekiel's story, especially as our modern world comes undone.

In the first three verses of Ezekiel's message, he describes how God awakened his desolate reality: "The heavens were opened, and I saw visions of God" (v. 1), then "the word of the LORD came . . . and the hand of the LORD was upon him there" (v. 3).

*Happy birthday, Ezekiel!*

The spectacular vision is, in many ways, hard to understand. But it was personally epic. Think of it. What's not hard to understand is that Ezekiel's exile led him into a profound God encounter. His sad solitude was gloriously disrupted by a massive wind, a bright cloud, lightning flashing, a fervent fire core, angelic creatures, spinning wheels, and above it all, a throne where mighty God appeared and spoke personally with Ezekiel.

God showed up in person, in Babylon, amidst dissonance and despair.

He still does.

The sacred presence of God, represented typically in the temple at Jerusalem, was transported to the dusty banks of the Chebar canal. Imagine it—your sorrowful thirtieth birthday celebration in a desert invaded by a personal visit from God. Ezekiel's darkest and most disastrous circumstances became his most profound and personal encounter with his Creator and Redeemer. How wonderfully unusual.

Every pastor desires the presence of God, but we generally seek the temple presence and do everything within our power to avoid the desert presence. We imagine the beautiful and never the barren. But the deep end of spiritual shepherding is about experiencing God in brokenness.

Ezekiel's astounding encounter announced an equally bizarre commission. He was assigned to deliver God's message to rebellious, unlistening people. In modern terms, *Go preach, speak . . . and fail.*

> EVERY PASTOR DESIRES THE PRESENCE OF GOD, BUT WE GENERALLY SEEK THE TEMPLE PRESENCE AND DO EVERYTHING WITHIN OUR POWER TO AVOID THE DESERT PRESENCE.

*Don't expect a welcome reception, attentive hearers, or responsive altar calls.* What about persuasive tactics and explosive growth hacks? Where are the trendy entertainment strategies and pithy communication tricks? Where is the promise of breakout revival?

Ezekiel's call was a paradox not only to his previous Hebrew experiences, but also to our modern ideas of gospel ministry.

Isaiah and Jeremiah were given similar assignments. Interestingly, it is highly probable that Ezekiel and Daniel knew each other and that both heard and received Jeremiah's preaching as young men. By modern metrics, Jeremiah was also a failure. For forty years his audience rejected, hated, and persecuted him. Yet, his faithful ministry sustained the few who listened—like Daniel and Ezekiel. Why did Daniel resolve to honor God (Dan. 1:9) and to maintain an "excellent spirit" (Dan. 5:12; 6:3)? Why did Ezekiel believe God was ordering his journey? Because Jeremiah's messages had prepared them both. Yet, Jeremiah never lived to see this wonderful fruit of his personal ministry.

The ripple impact of Jeremiah's faith-filled obedience is staggering. To the believing in Babylon, Jeremiah's and Ezekiel's prophecies would provide vital hope. *God is with us. He is faithful and sustaining us in this desolate place.* The invasion, the exile, the desert, the pagans, the scorn—God was active in it all, and He called His servants into it.

Have you ever considered the potential that your ministry journey could take you into similarly unimaginable circumstances or undesirable hardship? Does God still lead His shepherds into unwanted seasons of exile? Even more importantly . . .

*Would you still follow Jesus if you knew this is where He is leading you?*

## Small Ideas of Success

When we entered the ministry, we had an idea of what success would look and feel like—unwritten expectations. We imagined a desirable plotline—"a beautiful story for God." These imaginations are not evil, but they are flawed and insufficient. Hoped-for ideals are good things, but too often they are *ours*, and may or may not be God's. These predisposed ideas often come from good models we've experienced or studied—generally good places with good histories. The limitation of "case studies" is that they cannot be practically prescriptive for our journey, and they easily become idols.

With God's unusual call, one size does not fit all. Your journey is unique. Expecting any model to be duplicated is futile and frustrating. You and your assignment are distinct in God's design.

In every ministry leader's journey, there are unimagined and difficult realities that emerge. We anticipate our idea of success, but we are called to God's idea—which is often unlike anything we've imagined. To align with God's ideas, we must first lose ours. My preferred storyline rarely falls into sync with God's, and this misalignment results in a personal crisis—a critical impasse.

Whose version of the story will I chase? Do I pull the rip cord to escape God's uncomfortable script? Do I start over with a blank page? Or do I stay the course through the unexpected and dissonant chapters that God sometimes writes? Will I still embrace His version of the story when it becomes painful?

To dig deeper, our imaginations of success usually involve measurable things—conversions, baptisms, attendance, etc. Please don't misunderstand. These good fruits are wonderful and desirable, but they don't comprehensively quantify success in God's eyes. Who doesn't desire visible fruit? But who hasn't been tempted to manufacture it simply for the fleeting *feelings* or sense of accomplishment? We ought to pray, hope, and dream for evidential fruit, but more critically, we must deeply tie our hearts and hopes to simple obedience to Jesus.

It's enlightening to consider ministry results in biblical stories. Jeremiah or Ezekiel would have longed for a revival in Jerusalem or Babylon, but they never experienced one. Jonah literally attempted to thwart revival in Nineveh, but God moved mightily despite him. Go figure.

Bringing the idea into the present, healthy churches often experience spiritual fruit and fiscal blessing. But in what scope? When? How rapidly or slowly? And in what fashion does this materialize in a particular city, region, or context? In this light, visible metrics are not effective assessments of true, biblical success. God's work is His alone, and we are His servants. He does what He desires, and we only thrive when we rest more in Him than in results. Our deepest joy must flow from the gospel that holds us regardless of results (Luke 10:20).

Think about the subtle danger of manufactured success. Pre-boxed personal agendas divert us from the essence of our call. They tempt us to pursue our dreams "for God" rather than pursuing *Him*. They generate comparison and competition in our hearts. If our small, human-sized goals are achieved, we gravitate toward pride and become self-congratulatory and vulnerable to the many traps that success brings. Achievement grows into an idol that perverts our call and corrupts our souls. Alternately, if our goals do *not* materialize, failure threatens to break us with disillusionment. The resulting loss of identity drives despair and bad thinking, as well as the sense that we have failed God, and even worse, that perhaps God has failed us.

This subtle ministry idolatry is always oppressive. Man-made success subverts God's plan and drives us with unrealistic expectations and insatiable desires that lead to overwork and sick souls. It produces an ever-growing desire for more, but more is never enough.

## The Road to Disappointment

The loss of our ideals and expectations brings a kind of disappointment that legitimately threatens long-term wellness and fruitfulness. While every life faces disappointment, it is particularly inevitable in the heart of the pastor who is performance and productivity driven. What does this look like?

Generally, ministry leaders all face two types of personal disappointments—early and later disappointment, and we're ripe for both at different seasons. Go slowly here; it's important.

Early disappointment thinks, *This is not what I thought it would be.* This typically strikes when we are young and the work is more challenging and less emotionally gratifying than anticipated.

Later disappointment thinks, *I am not where I thought I would be.* These thoughts show up much later and evolve when our internal conversation is comparative.

Both kinds of disappointment are deadly if given the mind space to grow freely.

As a side note, all comparison is a head game. No matter your ministry metrics, someone has more. The social media stream faithfully dishes up posts of happier and more accomplished ministries. A steady heart rejoices in another's blessing, but a comparative heart devolves with envy and criticism. It's all purely subjective, and nobody is immune. A pastor of five thousand is as susceptible as a pastor of five. The only way to win is to refuse to play the game and to rejoice with *all* who are faithfully serving Jesus.

Personal disappointment is inevitable when our imagined stories conflict with God's greater story. This is when a critical question surfaces:

*Will I obey God if it means my script goes into the shredder?*

There is much mystery to the story God is writing with you. When, where, and in what ways He moves is His purview alone. His greater work is what He does within us, not only around or through us. Our primary role is not to manufacture a movement of God but rather to cooperate with Him in the ways He chooses to move. In light of His story, ours is always bigger than human eyes can see. Thankfully, God's idea of success is far more simple and more liberating than ours.

## God's Big Idea for Success

What is God's definition of success? What is so unusual about His call?

*Obedience is success.*

He calls us to obedience, not outcomes. This is counterintuitive to our achievement-based world. From the earliest of ages, we have been taught that success is results: grades, performance, wins, and eventually closed deals and financial gains. In God's unusual call, He ordains the outcomes and calls us to obey His directives. In love, we follow our Lord's simple instructions, repeatedly abandoning the lesser lords of personal achievement and formulaic success.

We fill the pots; He makes the wine. We hand over the lunch; He feeds the multitudes. We move the stone; He raises the dead. We cast the net; He loads up the fish. We step forward; He parts the sea. We step into battle; He fells the giant.

Or . . . we build the ark, and nobody steps aboard. We declare the message, and the hearers throw stones. We preach the gospel, and the world calls us fools.

Think of Ezekiel's and Jeremiah's decades of miserable ministry stats. Then think of Peter's and Philip's impressive growth trajectories in the churches at Jerusalem and Samaria. Or consider Paul's failing numbers in Athens in contrast to his stellar numbers in Corinth. God writes the story; we obey His directions.

When we embed our hearts in outcomes, we struggle for steady strength. When we embed our hearts in Jesus, that strength is inevitable. I love how C. S. Lewis put it in a letter to his friend: "It is not your business to succeed (no one can be sure of that) but to do right: when you have done so, the rest lies with God."[1]

Friend, God is writing a grand story, and your present chapter probably won't go the way you imagine it. The call requires deep surrender to mystifying circumstances, but "he who calls you is faithful; he will surely do it" (1 Thess. 5:24).

When you feel lost in a desert, God is closer than you realize.

The call to *obey* rather than *achieve* does not diminish the value, significance, or eternal implications of obedience. God always requires the surrender of personal ambitions—yes, even good desires. We abandon our purposes for His. We embrace the assignments He ordains and assume the roles He confers—even when they conflict with all preconceived expectations.

For this reason, I love the word "assignment." We don't manipulate His designs, we embrace and fulfill them. When the world shut down in 2020, like everybody else, I moped for a while. But in the middle of my self-pity, God dealt with my heart:

*Do you realize everybody on the planet feels this way? Have you considered that these events are My timeline for human history? Do you intend to sulk, or shepherd? Do you believe that I am active and advancing My eternal purposes? Undesirable circumstances are not disruptions or setbacks. This is your assignment. I sent you into this.*

I think I also heard a faint *Do. You. Love. Me?*

We each have our own difficult choice to embrace an undesirable exile.

May God's Spirit impress this resolve into your soul: *God placed me in this moment, in this place, for such a time as this* (Est. 4:14). *He sent me. This is my assignment. Success is obedience. God is active. I choose to find joyful fulfillment in simple obedience.*

## Embrace Paradoxical Success

God's call leads to places you never imagined and unfolds in ways you wouldn't choose. It disrupts your plan and devours your college dreams. He leads us through exiles and meets us on dusty riverbanks. We experience times when visible fruit is scarce, and obscurity is our closest friend.

His call requires deep abandonment of things that modernity dearly cherishes. God asks shepherds to do faith things (keep reading Ezekiel and you'll be thankful!). Our decisions to please Him will displease many. Though some will cheer us, many will criticize, gossip, or scorn us.

By virtue of the call, He requires wholesale surrender to these realities. Lay down your ideas and others' expectations. Follow Him above all models or mentors. Trust Him with a flying leap into oblivion. Get out of His way and let His story unfold, even when it's temporarily painful or ambiguous. Relinquishing autonomy to a loving Lord thoroughly contradicts the modern narrative of expressive individuality and self-determination, but it is profoundly healthy spiritually.

Perhaps this chapter is agitating or disruptive. Don't let it be. Releasing your *self* into God's story is liberating and lightening. It makes us free to follow Jesus in simplicity where we experience His gentle heart, light burden, and easy yoke (Matt. 11:28–30). This release puts us at rest—unencumbered by external or self-imposed productivity demands and freed to flourish in obedience. Only then can we love others purely—free from the temptation to exploit or objectify them in pursuing individualized vision.

When we finally accept the loss of self-made ideas, we can fall in love with God's version of the story. It's who we most truly are.

At some point, light will break through, and the barren riverbank will become an intimate God encounter. Our flying leap will land us in the soft center of His gracious hand. Whether next week or next decade, the page will turn, and a new chapter will be revealed. God's narrative will show that obedience was and is eternally and spectacularly fruitful. Only then will we discover how to understand the whys, cherish the hardness, and celebrate His paradoxical goodness.

In the gospel, clarity and joy eventually reframe every barren chapter of our stories.

One day we will celebrate the delight of simple, unquestioned *obedience*. In God's story, the hard always ultimately gives way to the amazing.

Right now, for the sake of sustained wellness, answer four questions. Revisit these when your heart begins to grow weary. Here they are:

- Am I where God has brought me in ministry?
- Is my present ministry what God knew it would be?
- Can I resurrender to Him right now?
- Will I choose to cherish the sheer joy of simple obedience?

If you followed God to where you are, then be there fully, even if it's complicated. If you didn't follow God to where you are, then quickly go where He calls you, whatever the cost. Trust Him in the unexpected. He is with you and will sustain you.

Steady strength is only possible if we can affirm this simple reality: *I am okay with however God chooses to write my story.*

The alternative is to live dangerously outside of God's authority.

It's impossible to serve Him by rebelling or resisting, and it's a quick way to break a church, hurt sheep, and self-destruct. Think of Jonah. God will work, but an uncooperative heart will experience His loving chastening.

## Moving Forward in Wellness

We are three chapters into the most philosophical and soul-searching part of this book—first seeking to build a strong core. Let's connect the ideas quickly.

**Decision #1: Embrace Insufficiency**—Our sense of weakness grows in proportion to our understanding of the depth and complexity of our spiritual responsibility. We are utterly dependent upon God's Spirit because the real work is infinitely beyond us. This can be a disheartening realization—*I can't do this.* Yes, that's step one. But quickly confess His infinite sufficiency. We are weak. He is strong. And His grace is always enough (2 Cor. 12:9).

**Decision #2: Seek Jesus**—Spiritual leadership grows complex and causes us to bounce haphazardly between three sets of expectations: ours, God's, and others'. The resulting ambiguity creates tension, stress, and internal confusion—*Who am I, what am I, and what am I supposed to be doing?* Therefore, we continually return to the essence—*I am a growing follower of Jesus. I love Him and am helping others to follow Him. My primary role is to feed His sheep.*

**Decision #3: Delight in Obedience**—Find great delight in *obeying* Jesus. Personal dreams fail us in disillusioning ways, but God's work continues forward. He works within us before He works through us, which means results are sometimes hard to see or track. This is out of sync with modern ideas of success. With Jesus, success is not outcomes; success is obedience—fully trusting Him to write the story.

Insufficiency is the reality of a strong core, loving and following Jesus is the function of a strong core, and delighting in obedience is the motivation of a strong core. This starting point of steady strength makes you free from impossible expectations, ambiguous job descriptions, and high-pressure productivity demands.

Ezekiel experienced an undesirable exile and a miraculous encounter with the living God simultaneously—we will too. Ultimately, his assignment wasn't his desired priestly office but rather the unexpected messenger to exiles. He was sent into Babylon for the glory of God—an unimaginable paradox to an ancient Hebrew.

Likewise, you are sent—divinely placed. Mourn the death of your imagined self, and pick up the truth of your God-called self, even in exile. Wherever you are, the heavens can open. You can know that God is always active in your life. The word of the Lord comes to you, and the hand of the Lord is upon you (Ezek. 1:1–3). Take heart in your desert.

As we turn the page—restful in our weakness, reminded of our first love, and released from personal agendas—we will turn our attention to a long-lost friend.

Next up, let's examine the *durability* of a strong core.

## CHAPTER FOUR

# THE GOOD NEWS LIFE

## CELEBRATE GOSPEL DURABILITY

*If God is for us, who can be against us? He who did not spare his own Son but gave him up for us all, how will he not also with him graciously give us all things? . . . In all these things we are more than conquerors through him who loved us.*

ROMANS 8:31–32, 37

As I write, I'm sitting on my back deck, a place where I've unpacked many complex problems with God. I'm fifty-three, but I feel thirty. The gray-bearded guy in the mirror surprises me. Dana and I have enjoyed more than three decades of marriage and ministry. The years evaporated so rapidly. How did three little kids grow up, graduate college, get married, and start families already? I've embraced the "Papa" identity with deep joy.

The story I see in the rearview mirror surprises me even more.

Most of this journey has been a complete surprise—right down to the writing of these words. And the surprises unfolded in both hard and happy ways.

We've explored how gospel ministry is challenging, but we're due for the alternate view. It's also an amazing good news life. Gospel-oriented leadership is derived from the good news, motivated by it, empowered by it, sustained by it, and designed to be dominated by it. The God-given theme of our souls is His good news. We are heralds of hope to captive hearts.

And we're not talking trivial or temporal good news.

## Immersing into Gospel Durability

We entered the ministry just months after we married and only days after we finished college. We relocated to assist friends in a rapidly growing church replant in the high desert of Los Angeles County. That assignment continued for twenty-two years and overflowed with opportunities, friendships, and joyful fruit. The ministry blossomed with new life by God's remarkable grace. The blessing and privilege of serving as an associate pastor would be hard to quantify briefly. God made those years exceptional in every way.

In September 2010, the story took a dramatic turn. Cancer was growing in five regions of my chest—stage 2B. It had been there for a year or more. I've written about this in the book *Off Script*,[1] so brevity will suffice. A motion-filled life essentially halted as we entered many weeks of tests, biopsies, and scans. Plans paused. Life was in limbo as survival was legitimately in question. By early November, we were informed that this cancer was likely curable with a year of chemotherapy and radiation.

Strange way to begin a chapter on "good news," right?

Well, these disrupting events almost immediately revealed something beautiful and wonderful about the presence and promises of Jesus.

Decision #4 is choose to *celebrate gospel durability.*

This is the experiential assurance that God's *good news* transcends all possible bad news.

This durability wasn't—and isn't today—self-willed or contrived. This was not the "power of positive thinking" or delusional optimism. We didn't dig deep to muster courage. This was much deeper than trying hard to see the bright side.

Jesus had already equipped our hearts for hardship in ways that surprised us but shouldn't have. Like Ezekiel's riverbank, God was there. He came to us and revealed the unspeakable power of His daily grace. We encountered unexpected durability that only the gospel brings to the soul.

We had heard of it for decades, but then we experienced it and knew with certainty it was not of ourselves.

Days after the diagnosis, I spent mornings slow reading the gospels. My prayer was, *Jesus, I need You, please give me a fresh view of Your heart.* The following day, I closed the last chapter of John. I wept with wonder at Jesus, mourned my subtle pharisaical tendencies, and celebrated the gospel at a new depth. In the shadow of death, my heart overflowed with delight in Jesus and the gospel.

Fighting and recovering from cancer continued for the next two years with a mixture of good and bad news—all undergirded by the *good news.* God did profound work in me and my family, both physically and spiritually. The first year was a slow crawl through treatments, alternating between being ill at home and having a minimally productive work life—bad news. The second year brought complete healing and a slow road back to physical strength—good news.

But as the first year ended, God also closed our California chapter of ministry. Seemingly bad news. He called us to a new assignment. Good news. He led us to a discouraged, declining church and Christian school in New England. Good but bad news. The small church family was eager to grow forward in gospel ministry. Good news.

Our relocation was both joyful and painful. We mourned letting go and saying goodbye. We grappled with profound disorientation and displacement. We feared and worried. Yet, with hope, we anticipated the new story God would write, believing He would change lives in New England. Our first six months in Connecticut brought a steady stream of bad news—from sad stories to financial struggles to decaying facilities to unjust critics.

As we entered the work, the challenges seemed insurmountable. Bizarre events repeatedly struck as if spiritual forces screamed, *Welcome to town, fools!*

Roof leaks flowed like garden hoses. Snakes crept into our basement. Random, cynical strangers verbally attacked us. On my first day in office, the church door fell off the hinges and nearly crushed the dear lady volunteering to clean restrooms. School parents I had never met were angry with me. Insidious criticisms were launched over email or online. Both friend and foe disseminated lies and false narratives. The list goes on.

Every day was a tug-of-war for my mind. I could focus on either stopping the gossip or spreading the gospel. More importantly, I could choose between justifying myself before others or the mission of helping others to be justified before God. The spiritual and mental battle was a moment-by-moment process that threatened to sicken my soul daily.

Strength and wellness flowed from choosing to live in the same gospel that I believed and preached. This is exactly what Paul meant when he wrote, "Now I would remind you, brothers, of the gospel I preached to you, which you received, *in which you stand . . .*" (1 Cor. 15:1).

These circumstances don't sound like a good news life.

But it *was.*

Many blessings arrived simultaneously. Every week about a hundred faithful people worshiped in a cavernous 1,100-seat room. New friends welcomed us with patient optimism. Faithful friends listened and responded to God's Word. Faithful believers gathered for evenings and mornings of prayer. Church family workdays yielded long-needed deep cleaning, full dumpsters, and organized closets. New hearts began to share the vision of a healthy, biblical church. A $20,000 monthly deficit diminished just in time.

But the best part—lost souls turned to Jesus one by one.

We had no money, no excellent programs, no beautiful facilities, and minimal music. We couldn't pay the bills. The ministry was six months from insolvency. Recovery was a week-to-week, day-to-day, nail-biting experience. I ping-ponged from flagrant faith in God to despairingly wishing I could fly away like a dove and be at rest (Ps. 55:6).

My younger, overconfident self would have thought, *C'mon . . . let's crush this!*

My recovering pharisaical, weak self was murmuring, *C'mon . . . this is crushing me!*

The only real hope we had was Jesus, the gospel, and prayer. And as our hearts were embedded with these three realities, we experienced again . . .

*Gospel durability.* His good news transcended all possible bad news. Jesus won. Jesus wins. And we win. I can hear you thinking:

*I know . . . Yeah, but . . . Cary—right now this is . . .*

The rebuttals swirl inside. I've been there.

*I know the gospel is good news, but this is dark. This is unfixable. This is impossible. This is stormy. This is overwhelming. This is breaking me. This is the one challenge that's finally going to outsize God.* We may not articulate it this way, but this is nearly the sense of it in our emotions and subconscious mind.

Is this breaking you, or is God breaking you? Big difference. Cancer did the halting. God did the breaking—but ever so gently. Recovery slowed life, but God did profound reshaping and calling. God ordained circumstances that led through deep valleys, but in them, He revealed the durability we actually (not theoretically) have in the gospel in those valleys.

We have to travel the valley to experience the durability.

In those valleys, like no other season in life, we cling desperately to the truth that His good news transcends all possible bad news.

The gospel not only transforms us, it transforms our problems as well. Essentially, the problems I thought were mine in actuality belonged to God, and in His hands they became something other than problems.

## Give Up or Go Deeper

Before you give up, God says, *Go deeper*. Like medicinal ointment, apply truth to the experience. Let Jesus move the gospel from your head to your heart. Allow great challenges to reveal a greater durability. Cooperate with God as He orchestrates a gospel encounter out of your overwhelming circumstances.

*He does the real work*. This is not only about knowing but also activating knowledge.

What if all the overwhelmingness of ministry could be downsized? What if all the overpowering challenges could be snowplowed into a big pile, zapped with a laser, and reduced to fit into a Tic Tac box? What if you could put it all into your pocket and enjoy a steady, joyful day? Wouldn't that be amazing?

When God sets you before an impossible assignment, He's not tormenting you (Lam. 3:33). He's subduing a smile and asking you a rhetorical question: *What are we going to do about this?*

He knows what *He* will do, but He's giving you a chance to faith—the verb. He's giving you a moment to put down fear and dream of impossibilities. He is the God of spectacular solutions.

What overpowers us doesn't so much as mildly alarm Him. Through the gospel, He invites us to be as unflinching as He is. "The worst they can do is kill your body"—so taught Jesus to His naïve disciples (see Matt. 10:28; Luke 12:4). Obviously, He was operating in a completely different headspace than we do. This is where He desires to lead us—unflinching durability and anticipatory dependence. *God, I can't wait to see what You have in mind here.*

In John 6:1–14, approximately twenty thousand people followed Jesus to a green field near the northeastern shore of Galilee and experienced His teaching and healing throughout the day. As the afternoon passed, they grew hungry, and there wasn't a Costco in town.

Knowing what He would do (v. 6), He asked Philip, who happened to be from nearby Bethsaida, "Where are we going to buy bread to feed all these people?" Do you see the subdued smile and wistful twinkle in His eye? Do you hear His inquisitive tone leading Philip toward expectant faith? To Jesus, a bread shortage is an opportunity. He is always good news to needy situations! But to Philip, breadlessness is an exasperating, anxiety-inducing impossibility.

Jesus sees only good news where we see only defeat.

Pause the video for a moment and think with me. Whose problem is this? Jesus' or Philip's?

We know it's Jesus' problem, but Philip owned it—or tried to. The correct answer for Philip, who had witnessed many miracles, would have been, *This is* Your *problem, not mine! Why don't You speak some food into existence, sort of like that wine thing at the wedding?*

But no. Philip took possession of the problem—first mistake. He broke out a calculator and spreadsheet and began doing math. A moment later, he threw up his hands in resignation. "We could work for two hundred days and only have enough money to buy one bite of bread for each person."

Philip led the scenario to defeat—game over—but Jesus was leading toward a miracle. He was just getting started! He's doing the same thing in your life right now. You may only see need and impending doom, but Jesus is setting up a marvelous, mind-blowing resolution.

He always takes His time, but then He always blows our minds.

Truth is, Philip should have immediately given Jesus His problems back.

Likewise, our sustained strength has everything to do with how we handle potential problems. Do we own and stew over impossibilities that ultimately only belong to Jesus? This devours enormous quantities of energy in our hearts and minds—we weren't designed for it. But as soon as we release and put the problems back on Him, they cease to be problems and immediately become opportunities— guaranteed eventual victories through gospel realities.

This is the very essence of His heart and promise in Romans 8:28 . . . *And. We. Know!*

## Remembering How Big God Is

Impossible things typically paralyze me at first. I deeply identify with Philip and other weaklings in Scripture. I instinctively calculate and deliberate like Gideon. Then I fear, worry, and mope a little—all of this consuming valuable emotion, time, and internal resources that should be given to other things—namely those I love and serve. Eventually, I give up in resignation with: "Lord, who do You think I am? I could work for two hundred days and still not solve all these problems."

Eventually, His good news begins to melt away my faithless exasperation.

His patient Spirit invites me to follow Him into a different headspace. It starts with solitude and His Word. Sometimes it involves mourning or airing my complaints like a psalmist. Then, God's presence, promises, and assurance begin to take control of the internal conversation.

Gospel theology soon invades my psyche, and Jesus' voice overpowers the inner cynic. His view breaks through—the hard work becomes *His*. The problems are *His*. This is going somewhere good because He is a good news God.

That knowing question arises again, *Cary, what are we going to do about this?* His nudge gently turns my heart toward His vastness.

He seems to ask, *Have you forgotten how big I am?*

The larger my view of Jesus, the smaller the problems and the more possible the impossibilities.

My first instinct should be, *Jesus, I can't wait to see what You're going to do with this disruption. Let me know my directive, but You do the heavy lifting.*

Too often, this is my eventual response rather than my first.

How I wish my first instinct would be, *Jesus, this is* Your *problem, not mine.*

All bad news bows before His good news.

Pastor Skip Heitzig once said it this way—"Difficulty must always be measured by the capacity of the agent doing the work!"[2] In light of Jesus' capacity, He has *no* problems. He's not worried, and He already knows what He's going to do to resolve our concerns.

When I'm trying breathlessly, God seems to ask, *Am I doing this, or are you?*

The gospel gives us the permanent answer—He has *done* and is *doing* the work!

Gospel durability infuses this truth: the gospel that saves us also secures us, shapes us, defines us, commissions us, and carries us safely home. The gospel places us in Christ and makes us the inseparable object of His unceasing good work. The gospel brings us into permanent granite-like stability with God, transcending all the shifting sands of life.

Our steadiness in Jesus is unmovable. "Therefore, my beloved brothers, be steadfast, immovable, always abounding in the work of the Lord, knowing that in the Lord your labor is not in vain" (1 Cor. 15:58).

> GOSPEL DURABILITY INFUSES THIS TRUTH: THE GOSPEL THAT SAVES US ALSO SECURES US, SHAPES US, DEFINES US, COMMISSIONS US, AND CARRIES US SAFELY HOME.

To Philip, feeding twenty thousand people is impossible, but what is it to Jesus? Fill in the blanks with your problems. What discouragement is pressing in? What loss is overpowering? What problems are overwhelming? What insurmountable walls threaten to crush you?

The gospel forever keeps the bad news from dominating our stories.

We are nevermore victims. We are not owned by nor defined by the broken or dark chapters of our lives. Death dies. Jesus wins. That's the ultimate happy ending of the good news story!

Think of the long journey ahead. What core reality will define you? What is the one thing in your life that is rock solid, unshifting, and always true? What truth can provide your core with evergreen strength?

Here it is:

You are a child of a good news God.

In Jesus, you are called to live a good news life.

You have been given a good news assignment.

God's good news transcends all possible bad news.

This is the foundation that you can rebuild on repeatedly. It never changes. Feel the thunderclap of this stability awaken you from a bad news stupor. Hear Him inquisitively suggest, *How are we going to feed all these people?* (Smile, wink . . .)

When looking at the state of this world, perhaps my words seem escapist or naïve. But if the gospel is true—and it is—then the good news life is the most rational form of living. Every adverse circumstance becomes granular in the shadow of grace. All the problems of life and ministry fit into a single Tic Tac box when exposed for a split second to this powerful question: *How does the gospel inform my understanding of this situation?*

## Durable Gospel, Fragile Child

God dropped weak me into a fragile ministry with many impossible challenges—a cancer patient partnered with a discouraged church family by God's providential assignment. What did He show us? The power of the gospel. As Jesus referenced in Luke 19:40, God could use rocks to declare the gospel. Yet He chose us and commissions us to live audaciously. He commissions good news lives in a bad news world.

The stories I've shared had positive outcomes over a long time—yours will too in the big picture. But don't miss this: gospel durability is most experiential—most tangible—when the results are not in yet. What if cancer hadn't been cured? What if the church had voted me out? What about when hard becomes harder? Remember the Hebrew children facing the fiery furnace? They declared: "Our God whom we serve is able to deliver us. . . . *But if not*, be it known . . . that we will not serve your gods" (Dan. 3:17–18).

The gospel doesn't just make you durable in the form of quick, positive outcomes. No, the gospel *is* the positive outcome and the guarantee of the ultimate outcome. The question is not, "Is the gospel durable?" but rather, "Will I choose to stand in it?" Will I so embed this truth that it becomes my heartbeat and dominant life narrative, even when deep waters don't recede? Peter calls it "the true grace of

God. Stand firm in it" (1 Peter 5:12). In Romans 8:31, Paul's troubles and enemies shrink when he declares, "If God is for us, who can be against us?" Then he celebrates, "In all these things we are more than conquerors through him who loved us" (v. 37).

What things? Hard things. Threatening things. Scary things. Impossible things.

How many times will we think, *Should I stick with this?* How many seasons of ups and downs will we travel through on this long road? We need one unshakable reality that repeatedly triumphs and renews steady strength in our lives.

*His good news transcends all possible bad news.*

Appropriate it every day. Make it your life theme. You are a herald of good news. You are not sent to fix all problems, answer all questions, right all wrongs, or execute all justice. You are sent to delight in, display, and declare God's good news in Jesus.

From every Scripture text—especially the ones on anger, justice, or hell—reveal the greater good news that God's holy diagnostic points to. In every circumstance—especially the impossible or despairing ones—bring the gospel into the equation. Be a distributor of hope and grace. This is the single soundtrack that Satan most desires to disrupt in our minds and ministries, precisely because it is the soundtrack that is most true, durable, and powerful. There is nothing we face that the gospel doesn't inform, recast, and ultimately overcome.

What a great privilege—we are good newsers! We share it, preach it, live it, and propagate it. But most importantly, we dwell in it. Living personally and intimately in that good news allows our souls to enjoy sustained wellness.

———

My oncologist became my good newser—Dr. Birhan, my Muslim friend, whom I have invited to believe in Jesus many times. In a sense, I owe him my life. I'll never forget when he told me my sickness could be cured.

We were viewing alarming scans and test results. After a few seconds, he looked at me and smiled. I thought, *How can he smile?* Then, with his distinctive Ethiopian accent, he made an almost prophetic declaration, "You've gotta find another way to die!"

When I paused, he repeated, "You've gotta find another way to die! This cancer is not going to kill you. We're gonna take over your life for one year. Then you're gonna be well and go pastor your own church somewhere!"

I laughed in mild denial but also rejoiced over the good news prognosis.

I was thankful for my unwittingly prophetic good newser.

My friend, *everybody* we shepherd is perpetually hammered with bad news. Everybody we could reach with the gospel is inundated with an ever-flowing stream of fearful, anxiety-saturated horrific news. The only answer the world provides is escapism—often self-destructive numbing mechanisms. These avoidance techniques teach us to pretend everything is better than it is. But eventually fake solutions are exposed and hearts once hardened to the gospel become thirsty for something true and durable.

The world needs joyful good newsers.

A strong core grows from a strong gospel. Jesus' good news makes us more buoyant than we could possibly feel or imagine. It's the reality that renews our strength over and over.

*Jesus loves me. He has done and is doing His work.*

We live in good news.

We grow in good news.

We declare good news.

## CHAPTER FIVE

# THE SOURCE OF STRENGTH

## GROW A GOSPEL IDENTITY

*Blessed are those whose strength is in you, in whose heart are the highways to Zion. As they go through the Valley of Baca they make it a place of springs; the early rain also covers it with pools. They go from strength to strength; each one appears before God in Zion.*

PSALM 84:5–7

The Greek poet Homer is famous for his eighth-century BC epic poems, *The Iliad* and *The Odyssey*. In *The Odyssey*, he wrote of a warrior sea captain, Odysseus. As Odysseus returned home to the island of Ithaca from the Trojan War, he and his crew sailed past the island of the Sirens. Homer described the Sirens as monstrous, murdering creatures who disguised themselves as beautiful mermaids to lure men ashore only to devour them.

As the myth goes, the goddess Circe warned Odysseus and his men to plug their ears with gobs of wax as they passed the Sirens. If the men couldn't hear, they wouldn't be enchanted by the tempting deception of the Sirens' calls. So, as the ship came into proximity of the island, Odysseus put wax in his men's ears, but left his own ears open. He desired to hear the Sirens for himself. To ensure his safety as they passed the Sirens, he instructed his men to take heavy ropes and bind him to the ship's mast. He told them not to free him under any circumstances, regardless of how forcefully he demanded.

As they passed the island, the men who could not hear saw the Sirens as hungry monsters. But to Odysseus, made insane by the enchanting songs, they seemed beautiful and alluring. Odysseus thrashed and screamed for release, but his men refused to untie him. Their resolve saved his life.

As they came to safety, the men finally unstopped their ears and unbound their captain. Now well past the island, Odysseus' senses returned, and he was thankful for the bindings that saved him during his madness.[1]

There is a similar kind of binding that saves us from our madness as well.

## Binding the Heart to Unfailing Realities

After three decades, nothing is more apparent to me than "My flesh and my heart may fail, but God is the strength of my heart and my portion forever" (Ps. 73:26). Like Odysseus, we must bind our hearts to truths that are stronger than the lies that mislead us and the emotions that disrupt us.

Steady strength is rooted in solid anchor points.

In this chapter, we will examine how to tie our hearts to a strong gospel identity. If our identity is tied to losable or changeable externals, our sense of self will be fragile. Likewise, it will be fragile if anchored to self-confidence or self-focused individualism. But Jesus offers a strong identity that binds our souls to truth and protects us from many moments of madness.

Before exploring this fifth decision of a strong core, let's connect the first four to it:

First, *we bound ourselves to His sufficiency versus our insufficiency.* This honest but hopeful encounter released us from artificially inflating or deflating our sense of self.

Second, *we bound ourselves to a personal love for Jesus.* We complicate what should be a delightful, organic relationship. We drift toward a job description over a personal relationship with Jesus. We forget we *love* Him. Jesus taught the abiding life in John 15:1–11 for this reason: "These things I have spoken to you, that my joy may be in you, and *that your joy may be full*" (John 15:11).

Third, *we bound our motives to simple obedience.* Pastoring is uniquely paradoxical in unexpected ways. Obedience is success. Laying down false expectations empowers and prepares us for unexpected assignments or exiles.

Fourth, *we bound our souls to durable good news.* This is both theological and personal as we incessantly inoculate our hearts with the gospel.

Now we examine the fifth element of a strong core—*gospel identity.* This is the emerging result of the first four.

### Slipstreaming

Aerospace engineers understand a dynamic called "slipstreaming."[2] A flying object creates a draft that produces forward momentum behind it. That momentum is moving at a similar velocity as the object itself. If another object moves into that slipstream, it can essentially rest in the energy created by the first. The front object bears the force of molecular displacement, while the one following can maintain the same speed as the first with far less exertion. The follower finds energized momentum in the slipstream of the leader. This is the operative principle when geese migrate in a flying-V pattern, or when a race car or cyclist drafts the vehicle in front of it.

What works for planes and geese also applies to leaders.

Jesus said, "Follow Me." He calls us into His slipstream. It's possible to be swept up into what Jesus is already doing and the momentum He is already generating, but it requires us to stay behind Him—to get into His flow.

Going solo is a heavy yoke. Moving out of the slipstream brings more friction and burns more fuel. Flying in the slipstream of Jesus is empowering and brings momentum that far exceeds what human effort could generate or sustain. He bears the brunt of the friction and brings continuous renewal of energy that provides sustained lift to otherwise weary wings. Slipstreaming results in steady progress that isn't nearly as demanding, and it allows for a restful, enjoyable labor—burden-bearing but not backbreaking.

This changes everything. From the lead position, Jesus takes the full force of ministry headwinds, which allows us to fly steadily and resiliently in His draft. For clarity, this is not us being infused with energy that makes us appear superhuman. No, it's the weak *me*—demonstrably weak—sustained by simply following in His wake. Imagine the sheer power of the slipstream of Jesus. How energizing and sustaining to live swept up by His momentum!

The slipstream of Jesus is where He exclusively determines our identity, assignments, direction, and decisions. He sets the pace, and we wholly subject our desires and goals to His momentum, which involves both losing and gaining—we lose our agendas, but we gain His strength.

Our passions push us insatiably harder and faster, but Jesus' draft provides three vital needs: *healthy restraint, sustainable flight,* and *clear direction.* Simply following Him makes way for all three.

Slipstreaming unshackles us from our forced attempts to write exceptional stories. It allows us to cooperate fluidly with His exceptional strength and greater story. Swallowed up in His glory, we soar with Him in restful unity, enjoying the journey rather than producing it.

When our identity is firmly bound to our Savior, the alluring pursuit of significance or affirmation is exposed as a deceptive monster. The madness of identity hunger is put to rest in Jesus, and spiritual sanity returns to the heart. Jesus releases our souls from struggle and purifies our motives to serve in love.

The challenge lies between doing God's work *for* Him (outside the slipstream) versus joining Him in work He is *already* doing (inside). Who's leading the effort, and who's following in the draft? Who is bearing the brunt of the burden, and who is riding the wave? To the casual observer, there may be no discernable difference, but the personal experience of the laborer in terms of exertion and energy is radically different.

The problem is that we often and gradually slip outside of Jesus' slipstream. Sometimes we even try to impress Him with our own: *Fly behind me, Jesus, and watch what I can do.*

## Serving *for* an Identity or *from* One

The world hammers us with nonstop identity messaging—*be an exceptional, remarkable high-producer.* Match this with the ever-present corporate ministry models that project larger-than-life images of "success." In the shadows, our averageness can seem pathetic. With echoes of pseudo-greatness taunting us, we wake up to our redundantly ordinary and unremarkable Monday mornings, depleted from Sunday, second-guessing our sermon, and already fielding inboxes rapidly filling with negative flow.

No wonder many under-shepherds fantasize about less complicated and more affirming vocations.

But the world's drive for "remarkable" is overrated and insatiable. It strikes at the core of our identity search. When living or serving outside of Jesus' slipstream, our identity need becomes maddening, like the temptations of Odysseus. The driven inner man presses us in ways that Jesus would not. The internal workaholic requires overextension, family neglect, and recurring depletion. But Jesus seeks to deliver us from this maddening, unfulfilling allure of affirmation or achievement.

When I entered the senior pastorate, I struggled with a dichotomy. My hungry work ethic collided with my diminished capacity. The urgent needs of a declining ministry exponentially outsized my post-cancer abilities. For many reasons, I was not the efficient, productive individual I strove to be for years.

We could say my sense of self was emaciated. To clarify, this wasn't a childish kind of trivial "me" trip. No, it was a deep sense of displacement and disorientation that everyone faces in dramatic seasons of loss or transition. I knew I was in God's will, but that call was uncomfortably at odds with the "me" I knew how to be.

Let's dig deeper here. What drove my desire for productivity and success? Were these good or evil desires? Primarily, the driver was love for Jesus and passion to serve Him. In part, it was a biblical work ethic. In part, it was love for the ministry and the joy of serving. There was also contentment in my comfort zone and sense of commitment—a deep devotion to God-given relationships and responsibilities.

However, subtly entangled with all these good things was also my flesh—a weak self, seeking an achievement-based strength. Good performance made me feel good about myself or gave me the sense that God was pleased. Therefore, *Who am I if I can't perform?* Our world programs us for this subtle behaviorism.

Performance-based cultures ceaselessly remind us that we are paid to produce, which drives us relentlessly. But in ministry, this mindset creates a low-grade soul tension because it is counter to the gospel of unconditional love. In a gospel-driven culture, we are loved and valued unconditionally because of Jesus' work, not our own. Therefore, our service flows *from* His love not *for* it.

In His mercy, God used my illness to begin delivering me from this unhealthy, performance-driven self (though it periodically shows back up). God essentially required me to watch the world function without me for a while. Then He led me into seemingly insurmountable challenges. At first, I was overwhelmed and played the victim. Imagine! I wondered why God was tormenting me, as did biblical authors (see Lamentations).

The flesh despises being bound to the mast of God's providence. Spiritual insanity loathes the loss of autonomy.

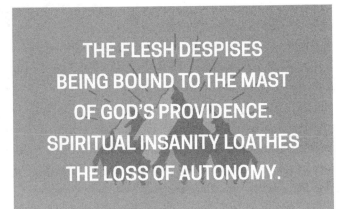

THE FLESH DESPISES BEING BOUND TO THE MAST OF GOD'S PROVIDENCE. SPIRITUAL INSANITY LOATHES THE LOSS OF AUTONOMY.

Gradually, Jesus convicted me of self-pity and gently coached me into His slipstream. It began with a prayer of surrender. A thousand problems swirled in my mind with no solutions. Formerly a performance-based junky, I was paralyzed by the impossibilities. My problem-solving skills were useless, and my psyche was sinking fast. My only option was like Peter's—"Lord, save me" (Matt. 14:30). This prayer was a desperate abandonment of self—an abdication of all rights to self-determination and self-dependence. It was a soulful admission that God's assignment had vastly outsized my performance capacities.

As always, the gospel came to the rescue once again.

From weakness, I prayed, "Jesus, do whatever You desire with this church and with me. You lead, I'll follow. Use my little contribution in whatever way You desire."

I had already felt like Philip saying with resignation, "We could never buy enough bread to feed all these people!" This weak-feeling prayer was perhaps a bit more like the boy. Thankfully, Jesus was not alarmed by my offer of a Lunchable.

Now, in my head, that prayer felt like failure. My success-conditioned psyche condemned me as a disappointment. *As God's problem-solver, I must be letting Him down.* In retrospect, that prayer was an imperceptible entrance into His slipstream.

God didn't unleash an immediate circumstantial transformation, but He did release my soul into a new, healthy trajectory. I began to cease striving *for* an identity and began to serve *from* one. I stopped expecting Jesus to do my will and bring forth my vision. I relinquished all expectations and focused exclusively on enjoying and following Him. Staying *behind* Jesus became my dominant life objective. Generating results or momentum ceased being *my* problem as I stopped bearing the burden of outcomes that Jesus alone produces.

His yoke is lighter and easier.

I stopped performing *for* Him and began to wait *upon* Him— seeking to move forward in sync and choosing to enjoy the journey and savor the view from behind. It was then that the work of ministry ceased being an overburdened, overextended life. God did the heavy work. Jesus became chief problem-solver, and I tagged along in the easier side of the yoke. At least this is the goal.

Slipstreaming.

This way of laboring with Jesus is less effort, more fun, and beautifully fruitful on His terms. It is life-giving. It yields up restful service and joyful productivity—energizing from a heart filled with His abundance. This means the search for fullness has successfully come to an end in Him.

A strong identity makes us free to love and serve from fullness rather than for it.

Your true identity in Jesus immerses you so completely into infinite grace that you can enter every ministry space seeking to distribute grace rather than expecting to receive it.

Slipstreaming operates from wholeness rather than seeking to find it.

His draft is accessible to you right now.

## Receiving a Strong Identity

"Come to me, all who labor and are heavy laden, and I will give you rest. Take my yoke upon you, and learn from me, for I am gentle and lowly in heart, and you will find rest for your souls. For my yoke is easy, and my burden is light" (Matt. 11:28–30).

We *believe* this passage but do we experience it? Is it possible to find that space where serving Jesus is easy—not just conceptually but really? This almost sounds heretical to a culture where living on "the ragged edge" is viewed as noble martyrdom.

How does *easy* jive with running our race (Heb. 12:1–2), pressing on toward the goal (Phil. 3:14), striving together for the faith (Phil. 1:27), devoting ourselves to the ministry (1 Cor. 16:15), and working night and day (1 Thess. 2:9)? What's the balance formula that brings the concept of hard work and the shalom life together?

Practically, how do we expend ourselves in restful ways?

What does the slipstream experience look like?

The bottom line is that our identity-starved inner person drives us much harder than Jesus would. The experience begins by *coming to Him* with our heavy-burdened, hard-working selves. Sounds like the typical pastor, doesn't it? It's comforting to realize Jesus understood that the gravitational pull of our flesh is drivenness in search of identity.

When we come to Him heavy and burdened, His immediate response is, *You need rest.* Jesus is a rest-giver, not a slave driver. He is opposed to the inner-identity drive that holds the gun to our heads. He's no oppressor.

If you are exhausted and depleted (now or perpetually), Jesus isn't creating that condition. His expectations do not press or stress us. We run very hard following a Savior who walked less than 3 mph everywhere He went! This begs the question: Whose demands drive us in our sustained states of overextension?

The answer is always horizontal—ourselves or others. Usually, it's both. Who are we laboring to please? Whose affirmation and acceptance are we striving for? Who is setting our pace?

In the gospel, we already have all of Jesus' acceptance.

Thankfully, when we come to our senses and come to Him, His response is gentle.

*Whew!* Repentance brings relief rather than rebuke. We discover Jesus is not wringing His hands in distress or rage. He is our safest haven, but His very next directive is where we struggle and where we find out whose demands drive us.

His invitation is more than a salvation opportunity. It is also an identity opportunity.

"Take my yoke upon you."

It sounds simple enough, but it's a big deal. His implication is: *Receive My design of you. Accept My definition and shaping of your story. Enter My call and assignment for you. Follow My direction and fly in My slipstream. Relinquish your right to self-determination and link up to true discipleship.*

The phrase identifies good labor—a yoke—a healthy, productive kind of service rendered in love and valued by Jesus. But He calls us away from heaviness; it's His yoke, and He's in it with us. He's the stronger co-laborer.

Our flesh is subtle. Even though our self-imposed yokes are heavy, we don't like to relinquish them. They've become so familiar we hardly realize how crushing they are. We have developed "learned helplessness"[3] in our captivity. Our depleted, exhausted selves have become our version of *normal*, and we feel stuck with a heavy identity—which is far better than the unbearable thought of *no* identity. Losing our burden is unthinkable because it is so inextricably tied to our sense of identity.

The heavy yoke is the achievement-based identity we strive to sustain. By contrast, His easy yoke alleviates the work and confers a true, grace-based identity. In unconditional love, He provides all the affirmation, acceptance, and significance our hearts could desire—forever. This gospel-shaped self is full and cannot be lost, which profoundly transforms our core desires. When we serve *from* a strong identity, we engage in life-giving ministry that energizes more than it depletes.

Finally, Jesus' phrase invites decision and action. We *receive* this yoke. We don't make, create, define, or manipulate it. We come to Him and enter into it. We bow our knees and submissively allow Him to generously confer it upon us.

Decision #5, *grow a gospel identity*, is a sacred and wonderful journey.

I love the phrase, "Learn of me." In this yoke, we are learners, and He is our teacher. The slipstream won't come instinctively, but it can be learned over time. The evidence of progress is our emerging heart of gentleness and humility—He is "gentle and lowly in heart." The unavoidable result of His easy yoke is a restful soul that handles His sheep with gentleness versus dominance.

## Embrace Gospel Identity

The dissatisfied inner man must be held to account. He is living under a heavy yoke imposed by others and himself. That devious flesh loves to blame-shift or play the victim of others or circumstances. In reality, he's the one holding the gun to your head, and he is you.

The only alternative to this madness is to be tightly bound to Jesus' yoke. Our internal longing for significance and validation can be found exclusively in Jesus. Surrendering to Him calms the soul's breathless quest to *achieve*. Once surrendered, our quieted hearts can restfully *receive* the redeemed self that Jesus confers by grace.

He always does more with us in our restful surrendered state than He can in our self-assured, driven state. He actively opposes this prideful lifestyle (1 Peter 5:5). Peter's usefulness at Pentecost was a product of his John 21, failure-saturated surrender, not his John 18, sword-swinging bravado.

To personalize these thoughts, can you appropriate the gospel's answer to these questions at a soul level?

Who does Jesus say I am?
Why does Jesus accept me? (Works or grace?)
To what extent does Jesus love and affirm me?
What has Jesus created and called me to do?
Am I laboring for a strong sense of self or from it?

A gospel identity is the yoke that makes us free to be who Jesus says we are. He liberates us from our thirsty imaginations and others' unattainable or unsustainable expectations. Jesus releases us into a restful, easy yoke as our true Shepherd and Friend.

To grow a gospel identity is to lose or relinquish who you thought you were and enter into who Jesus shaped you to be. It frees your psyche from living up to the demands of others or yourself and enables you to enter His gentle shaping of your true self—to become the you God has in mind in Christ. It is not expressive, radical individualism (*I just gotta be me*), but it isn't enslaved conformity either (*I have to gain everybody's approval*). This is the loss of renegade self-determination for the reality of true and God-given uniqueness and validation. From this wellspring of meaning and provision, we become free in self-giving, difference-making service in His name.

Gospel identity sets down egoism and picks up humility. It devalues personal achievement and self-glory, and highly values private obedience for God's glory and others' good. It relinquishes individual liberty for the sacred privilege of influence. It trades hard labor for energizing effort flowing organically and joyfully from our God-given design.

This is the delighted, restful, unburdened version of you that everybody wishes would show up more often. It's a gospel-shaped you—unique but like Jesus in authentic ways. This is you becoming like Jesus in what seems like an almost effortless way—it's growth that shows up and surprises you because you didn't work at it, and you didn't recognize it until someone else noticed. We can cultivate this, but we can't manufacture it. We can abide in it, but we can't fake or force it. It can materialize, but it can't be fabricated.

Ministry is designed to flow from a strong identity, not to provide one. Yet we tend to subconsciously drift toward seeking a personal identity from ministry and from the affirmation of people, the gratification of achievements, or the pride of individualism. Spiritual leadership is intrinsically designed to be self-giving rather than self-centered—we are caregivers before we are care-receivers.

Using the church family as a source of identity is not a new concept. The early church pastor Augustine of Hippo described the same alluring temptation centuries ago: "Now I see many adulterers who desire to get possession of the bride, purchased at so great a price . . . and those adulterers strive with their words to be loved instead of the bridegroom."[4]

He went on to describe how detestable a man would be to attempt to win the heart of his friend's bride. The true Groom, Jesus, has committed His bride to our care, not so we can win her affection, but so we can guard and fuel her affection for Him.

A gospel identity makes us so complete in Jesus that we can rejoice that the bride supremely loves Jesus and appropriately esteems her under-shepherds. As J. C. Ryle wrote, "Every faithful minister . . . must be content to be less thought of by his believing hearers, in proportion as they grow in knowledge and faith, and see Christ Himself more clearly."[5]

This Sunday, you will stand before Jesus' bride and minister to her. Look around the room. Consider the hearts. See the faces of God's sheep. Ask yourself, "Am I seeking to feel better about myself? Or am I seeking to feed these souls? Who's the hero? Am I seeking something for me? Or am I serving Someone in sincerity?"

Like Odysseus should have done, plug your ears to the temptation of fragile identity. Bind your flesh to the mast of Christ's love and relish His infinite affirmation of your truest self. By faith, step into the fifth decision of a strong core—celebrate gospel identity.

"Be strengthened by the grace that is in Christ Jesus" (2 Tim. 2:1).

Take off the heavy yoke. Step into the easy.

Welcome to the slipstream!

*According to the riches of his glory he may grant you to be strengthened with power through his Spirit in your inner being.* Ephesians 3:16

# Part Two

# NURTURE A FLOURISHING SOUL

## 6 Practices That Renew and Sustain Strength

*The LORD is my strength and my shield;*
*in him my heart trusts, and I am helped. Psalm 28:7*

How can we maintain the strong core we've studied? What does soul maintenance look like?

A sick soul is a contagion. Pastors don't produce what they *want* but organically reproduce what they *are*. As a sick soul is transmissible, so is a flourishing soul.

God's people deserve healthy shepherds who live from healthy souls. Yet, it's the most devoted, hardworking hearts that are also the most likely to burn out.

As the gatekeeper of your inner man, you cultivate the health that becomes your culture. Your wellness impacts many. For their sakes and our own, let's examine six soul-nurturing practices:

*#1—Counterbalance Negative Flow*
*#2—Maintain a Sustainable Pace*
*#3—Pursue Body and Brain Wellness*
*#4—Nurture Healthy Relationships*
*#5—Open Up to Real Friends*
*#6—Enjoy Solitude with Jesus*

*My flesh and my heart may fail, but God is the strength*
*of my heart and my portion forever. Psalm 73:26*

## CHAPTER SIX

# LIFE-GIVING OR LIFE-DRAINING

## COUNTERBALANCE NEGATIVE FLOW

*But we have this treasure in jars of clay, to show that
the surpassing power belongs to God and not to us.*

2 CORINTHIANS 4:7

I ran out of gas on the way to perform a wedding. Humiliating. Not
when I was a new driver. Not years ago. *Recently.* After nearly four
decades of driving as an adult, I . . . well, I can't bring myself to write
it again. You know.

Here are the brutal details. It had been a busy weekend moving from
one meeting to the next. In the hurry, I kept noticing my gas gauge was
low, and each time I thought, *Gotta get gas, but not now . . . later.*

This happened no less than four times between Saturday morning
and Sunday night.

As Monday morning arrived, the fuel gauge talked to me. *Hey,
doofus—this is your last chance to fill up before driving to the wedding
later today. You can't forget.*

In a rush I thought, *I'll remember to get it on the way*. Big mistake.

As my morning meetings wrapped up, I changed clothes, picked up my wife, and left for the much-anticipated event with friends. Thinking of my wedding remarks and enjoying the conversation with my wife, fuel was the last thing on my mind at that point. We drove, talked, and enjoyed the beauty of the Connecticut countryside in fall . . . until we didn't anymore.

The car sputtered, stalled, and coasted to the side of the road as my heart raced.

"I'm an idiot!" I shouted to my wife's puzzlement. "I just ran out of gas. I can't believe I did this!"

Her response was pity—the kind you feel for a pathetic person. *This poor, pathetic, busy, aging man . . .*

Immediately I was calculating time while imagining the endless flak friends and family would deliver. I deserved it. *They will never let me live this down.* As of this writing, they haven't. In fact, on the day of my own daughter's wedding a year later, the father of the groom texted me asking, "Hey, do you need me to bring a gas can?"

Fortunately, we had forty-five minutes of margin, but we were dead in the water and still twenty minutes from the venue. This gave me a window of time to recover, and we had passed a gas station about a mile back. With one phone call, my oldest son, Lance, was on his way with a gas can, plenty of ribbing, and a ride to save the day. We pulled into the event with three minutes to spare.

For the next week, whenever I called my son's cellphone, he answered by saying, "I got you, Dad. Where are you? I'm on my way!"

I guess the laughs made the ordeal worth it.

## The Paradoxical Negative Flow

Every aspect of ministry is either life-giving or life-draining—restoring strength or burning it. This is true of people, activities, projects, and environments. It's impossible to give out what we don't first receive, and we can never give more than we have in reserve.

Are you aware of which dynamics *consume* resources and which *replenish* them in your unique context? Do you give attention to your spiritual, emotional, and physical energy gauges—ensuring that you refuel more than you burn?

There's a reason why this is a significant struggle for spiritual leaders.

How can such a joyful, life-giving call simultaneously involve such life-draining depletion and emotional expenditure? If emotional energy were physical fuel, real gospel ministry is a gas-guzzler—for both positive and negative reasons.

I have wrestled with this chapter for months. It's hard to wrap my mind around the paradox of blessing and burden that comes with ministry. I've considered writing it on Monday mornings, but I don't want to depress you.

On the one hand, pastors experience immense joy and privilege. We love what we are called to do. On the other hand, we experience a steady, brutal flow of negativity. Ministry involves a stream of soul-depleting dynamics that are difficult to understand and manage.

We regularly swim in a negative flow of life.

No complaint here; it's what we signed up for. But if we don't understand and manage it courageously, it will swallow us and our families. Any version of people-work includes this stress and therefore sustained health must account for it.

After serving as an associate pastor, I wasn't surprised by the stress headwinds the senior leader faces, but the art of counterbalancing it proves challenging. Too much negative for too long, without a counter-balance, sucks the life from your heart and makes you imagine a less problem-centric vocation.

Pastors deal with large quantities of distress. Like trauma professionals, hospice workers, or first responders, we absorb a steady diet of human suffering, raw emotions, and dark experiences. We see life and people at their worst on a regular basis, often bearing the brunt of brutal emotions in the form of criticism.

Hurting people hurt people, and the pastor is sometimes the one they punch. We step into a negative river each morning and swim upstream much of the time. When someone requests to talk to the pastor, it's likely that everything is falling apart, and the pastor is expected to provide a quick fix. Plus, these are problems bad enough that no one else wants to touch them.

For this reason, our daily reality is often light on levity and heavy on crisis. Large portions of our workweek can be devoted to urgent problem-solving involving heavy implications. This steady imbalance toward intensity, negativity, and stress is significant, and unaddressed or unmanaged, it can exact a heavy toll on our hearts, personality, and relationships.

Add to this the intrinsic hardship of daily spiritual battle and you have an intense formula for personal drain or discouragement.

I have felt this stress change me in concerning ways. My light-hearted, optimistic self can be subtly weighed down with negatives that are consuming my mental bandwidth—which is unfair to family and friends and unsustainable personally.

Additionally, we are *people workers*. We expend ourselves emotionally and relationally with great intensity. We can't choose to "not care"—but caring becomes *carrying*, which becomes *consuming*. It's difficult to learn how to care without carrying or being consumed by the cares.

Though a privilege, this dangerous combination—negative flow + extreme expenditure—sets up a recurring worst-case scenario that leads to soul exhaustion. Spiritual leadership is predisposed to spiritual burnout.

Our daily news stream goes something like: "Pastor, my husband left me." "Pastor, my doctor called." "Pastor, I just lost a loved one."

"Pastor, I'm irritated with you because . . ." As I was writing this, one call among a hundred others was, "Pastor, the school is on fire!"

One time a man said to me, "Pastor, I need to apologize for hating you for the last ten years." Honestly, I could have gone without knowing. This sort of thing is no longer surprising. Bizarre and weird, yes. But not surprising.

Spiritual and emotional warfare is exhausting. In my experience, a thirty-mile bike ride is less tiring than preaching twice on a Sunday morning. A one-hour workout is less draining than thirty minutes of spiritually intense counseling. Pastoral ministry consumes soul resources like fast-burning rocket fuel—a dynamic that is unique, invisible, yet physically and emotionally real.

The negative flow makes our lives lopsided with adverse intake—a steady diet of hardship—and it creates an emotional PTSD experience over time. Something as simple as an email or text message can evoke a pang of anxiety about yet another potential crisis. These pangs are like low-fuel warning lights on the dashboards of our souls.

Of course, there are many joyful, offsetting positives. "Pastor, I trusted Jesus today." "Your message helped me." "Our family is growing." And for most engaged pastors, this too is a steady stream. Every week we experience both streams simultaneously, but too often the former is a deluge, and the latter is a trickle.

Much of the negative flow arises from the privilege of shepherding wounded and struggling sheep. Spiritual growth and disciple-making is a wonderful but messy process. God's people, including us, are needy; and gospel ministry is about giving comfort, showing mercy, extending grace, and helping hearts. Therefore, we consume large doses of desperation and burn through many fuel tanks of mercy.

As we are "helpers of . . . joy" (2 Cor. 1:24 KJV), we are also *absorbers of pain.*

The inevitable emotional depletion leaves us with nothing left to give—a serious and unsustainable reality. In a world where extreme overextension seems to be the very definition of success, we don't have the option of serving from emptiness. The stress drain imprints our souls and shapes our psyches, and it demands counterflow and intentional soul care.

Healthy pastors refuel often and abundantly. They pursue practices, construct schedules, and nurture relationships that fill the same fuel tanks that ministry rapidly burns through. As we are expenders of grace, we must be even greater consumers of grace.

## Finite Creatures Serving Infinite Needs

We were created as finite creatures—"jars of clay" (2 Cor. 4:7) with limited emotional and physical capacities—serving an infinite stream of needs. A paradox. Our work is never done, and ministry growth only increases the needs to meet—both an awesome privilege and a strategic challenge.

How do we sustain wellness in a notoriously draining vocation?

Remember, ours is a good news life! We are called to lead God's people into flourishing, celebrative living. *But how can we help others flourish if we aren't flourishing ourselves?*

The math is simple: positive input must outweigh negative expenditure. Refueling must outpace fuel burn, and generous margins are vital. If the negative flow is granted indefinite burn time, burnout is unavoidable. Given reasonable margins, we can all sustain imbalance for a time—everyone runs on reserves or fumes occasionally—but no one can do so indefinitely.

Too much for too long means emptiness is getting that much closer.

Balancing the flow—positive versus negative—should be simple, but it is incredibly complex. The bottom line is: if the demands of the ministry consistently exceed the resources you possess to meet them, your service is not sustainable.[1] Thirty minutes of fuel is never going to take you an hour's distance.

The secret is in monitoring your spiritual, emotional, and physical fuel tanks and filling the tanks often enough to stay ahead of the expenditure. It's not rocket science.

Pause to refuel as often as required to press forward faithfully. It really is that simple. But it isn't. We feel the burn, but we always think we can eke out a few more miles. There are always more needs to engage, and downtime often feels selfish or almost like a betrayal of our calling.

Going the distance will require strategic attention to two factors:

- The pace of burn—How quickly are you expending personal resources?
- The frequency and quality of refueling—How often and how effectively do you restore your whole being?

It is our human propensity to treat ourselves as unlimited resources or to be oblivious of our refueling needs holistically. We want to be everything to everyone, and we subtly believe that soul and body neglect is somehow the built-in cost. This thinking exposes a subtle god complex. God graciously disrupts our attempts to be infinite by imposing human limits and requiring us to surrender to those limits. God-given limits free us from the soul-destroying burden of playing God.

> GOD-GIVEN LIMITS FREE US FROM THE SOUL-DESTROYING BURDEN OF PLAYING GOD.

We can only do, endure, absorb, and process so much, so it all comes down to how we strategically budget ourselves.

But how do we allocate or monitor invisible, emotional, and spiritual assets?

Begin with this affirmation—God never asks us to expend more energy than He provides. Choosing to live within His imposed limits is an act of humility, trust, and submission. It releases us to answer life's hard questions with courage:

Is God holding it all together, or am I?

Am I trusting Him by embracing my limitations?

How does God desire to allocate my inner resources?

Are those resources being refueled at a faster rate than their depletion?

Are my internal resources expended in ways that are most essential?

Am I regularly neglecting the refueling of any part of my being?

Am I willing to recognize and admit when I'm approaching empty?

How do we consistently replenish ourselves from the living wellspring of Jesus (John 4:14; 7:37–38)? First, let's find good company in the struggle. Then, in the following chapters, we will explore six practices that counter the burn with substantive refueling.

## Finding Good Company in Negative Flow

The apostle Paul experienced exhaustion and emotional depletion more than once. He traveled through several seasons of personal distress or depression, and he transparently wrote of them.

On his second journey, the Lord redirected his travel plans in Asia, routing him to Troas in eastern Turkey and then across the Aegean

Sea into Macedonia, present-day Northern Greece. Both blessings and burdens awaited him in this new region. Paul was beaten and imprisoned at Philippi and then rejoiced as God turned sorrow to joy and a new church was born. He then narrowly escaped assaults and threats after a short but fruitful stay in Thessalonica and Berea. To spare his life, his friends sent him away on a boat heading south.

Arriving in Athens, Paul was low on every resource. He was alone, drained, out of money, and short on visible hope. He encountered much scorn, saw little fruit, and decided to journey to the larger city of Corinth to the west. Writing from Corinth to his friends in Thessalonica, he described his emotional state of distress: "Therefore *when we could bear it no longer*, we were willing to be left behind at Athens alone . . ." (1 Thess. 3:1–8). Desperate to reconnect and strengthen his new believing friends in Thessalonica, he sent Timothy and Silas to minister to the afflictions that had befallen them all. The unstated question is, *Who ministered to Paul?*

In verses 3 and 4, he qualified the anguish, "We are *destined* for this . . . to suffer affliction." He went on to describe the season again as unbearable (v. 5).

Inner depletion truly makes us feel unable to bear it—a sort of living death, a slow trudge forward in the dark that breeds deep discouragement—from cynicism and despair to anger and doubt. Self-cynicism is one of the surest signs of the soul's depletion.

Verses 6–8 pull the curtain of his experience back further:

But now that Timothy has come to us from you, and has brought us the good news of your faith and love and reported that you always remember us kindly and long to see us, as we long to see you—for this reason, brothers, in all our *distress* and *affliction* we have been comforted about you through your faith. For now we live, if you are standing fast in the Lord. (1 Thess. 3:6–8)

Did you catch the reference to distress and affliction? When arriving at Corinth, he was in a very dark place experientially. It's important to note Paul was spiritually strong but emotionally depleted. Paul's faith was intact, his mission clear, and his devotion secure. Yet, his inner strength and personal resources were spent beyond human ability to sustain. Something had to give.

Acts 18 tells more of the story. In his low place, Paul rationed his energy, ministering only one day a week, teaching in the synagogue in Corinth. He took a full-time job in a leatherworks shop making tents with Aquila and Priscilla, a displaced couple from Rome. This was a low and lonely season for Paul, but God was beautifully at work in ways only *waiting* would reveal. He waited out the weariness.

Likewise, God is beautifully at work in our dark or lonely places. Patiently waiting on Him, and restoring our souls in Him and in practical ways, will ultimately lead into His larger story. Sometimes God's seasons of forced waiting are His greatest gift to us. He may be renewing us in ways that only time will reveal. Consider how God worked in Paul's situation.

First, Aquila and Priscilla became believers and devoted gospel partners with Paul. They served churches in multiple locations for many years, and it all began in a low season when Paul was seemingly sidelined from full-time ministry.

Second, good news was on the way from Thessalonica. In a day when travel was difficult, it took Timothy and Silas weeks or months to journey from Thessalonica to Corinth. Their reunion is recounted in Acts 18 and 1 Thessalonians 3. Their presence infused Paul with an immediate resurgence of energy. The generous offering and the good reports they brought from Christians in Northern Greece revived Paul's passion. At this point, he resumed preaching the gospel full-time.

Thirdly, and most beautifully, Jesus personally relieved Paul's anxieties. As Paul reengaged in full-time gospel ministry, he probably suffered from a form of PTSD related to past persecution. Jesus understood this and personally ministered to Paul in a dream. He conferred courage and strength and calmed his natural human anxieties: "Do not be afraid, but go on speaking and do not be silent, for I am with you, and no one will attack you to harm you, for I have many in this city who are my people" (Acts 18:9–10).

In his soul's darkness, rather than self-destruct, Paul responded cautiously. He relocated to a beautiful city on the Mediterranean and the Ionian Sea. He maintained a steady work life and waited on God's restorative resources. During that low season, God providentially renewed Paul and continued working in the background. He restored and prepared Paul for the next phase of life. He resourced Paul with a restful pace, a small community of new believing friends, physical provision, and meaningful diversionary work. In time, God brought a team, financial resources, and spiritual renewal. The season refueled Paul with spiritual energy to preach Jesus, emotional margin to process anxiety or opposition, and physical strength to serve with daily passion.

He wrote of his emotional journey as being "afflicted in every way, but not crushed; perplexed, but not driven to despair; persecuted, but not forsaken; struck down, but not destroyed; always carrying in the body the death of Jesus, so that the life of Jesus may also be manifested in our bodies" (2 Cor. 4:8–10).

Paul then stated, "So we do not lose heart. Though our outer self is wasting away, our inner self is being renewed day by day. For this light momentary affliction is preparing for us an eternal weight of glory beyond all comparison" (vv. 16–17).

Later, during his third journey, Paul became so deeply depressed that he entered dark despair and expected to die. In 2 Corinthians 1 and 2, he referenced the affliction he experienced in Asia, explaining that he was burdened beyond human ability. His anguish was so intense that he could not preach the gospel in Troas, though a great door was opened. This is the only time in Paul's ministry where he shared that emotional factors prevented him from preaching Christ in an otherwise open opportunity.

If Paul dealt with emptiness, we will too. Truth makes us free and empowers us to reckon with the normalness of soul depletion and to realize that God's grace grants us permission (and, in fact, encourages us) to sustain and live within healthy margins.

## Don't Be Captain Fumes

I shouldn't have run out of gas. The gauge was screaming at me for two days. Thankfully, the situation was recoverable.

Unfortunately, I've run out of gas spiritually, emotionally, and physically many times. At first, I thought it noble. Then I reckoned myself deficient. Eventually, I began to see the pattern—from expenditure into depletion into restoration. But here's the key:

*Why not lose the depletion component?*

The goal for sustained health is to move from expenditure to restoration and back to expenditure. As we learn this recurring pattern, the situation is always manageable and recoverable. While not always possible, this is the goal. Sometimes depletion sneaks up on us unpredictably, in which case the challenge is recognizing and responding to it with humility and courage.

If you permit it, the negative flow will drain you and change you. From empty fuel tanks, your skewed perspective will immerse you in dark emotions and transform you into a cynical, agitated leader. It will become increasingly harder to "put on a happy face."

I'm still seeking to understand this fluid dynamic. It is complex. It's a daily tension to manage, not a problem to solve.

Gospel ministry provides us the amazing privilege of entering the distress of others. We care for their souls, feel their burdens, walk through their valleys, and nurture their hearts. We weep with those who weep—a lot. To continue serving in this privilege, we must refuel—counterbalance the rapid burn of negative flow. In these situations, we are essentially sharing our oxygen masks and allowing others to burn our energy.

Better have some backup oxygen tanks!

If we don't account for this extra burn and renew more often, we'll soon be broken.

One thing I didn't share about the wedding story—the car stalled on a busy two-lane route with almost no shoulder. For twenty minutes, we sat halfway on the road—an awkward, dangerous predicament that could have gone horribly wrong. Hoping to ensure visibility to those traveling at high speeds around the nearby bend, I stood by the car looking pathetic.

Nobody stopped. The funny thing is, even good friends drove right by on their way to the wedding. We laughed later that they were so focused on not hitting us that they didn't even notice it was us!

Don't play flippantly with empty. Don't try to be Captain Fumes. It's not only miserable but also risky! Your friends will think you're nuts and will miss the better version of you.

Take inventory. What aspects of your role are life-draining, and what practices are life-giving? What burns energy and what refills the tank? Begin building a positive flow that offsets the negative. Your long-term ministry health depends on it. My pastor friend, Scott, says it this way, "Do whatever you have to do to keep doing what God has called you to do."

Begin habits of refueling long before bottoming out in depletion. Live with margin, and when you can't, stop and restore your resources as quickly as possible.

Nurturing Practice #1 is *counterbalance negative flow.*

Everything ahead will help us do just that.

## CHAPTER SEVEN

# LESS IS MORE

## MAINTAIN A SUSTAINABLE PACE

*He makes me lie down in green pastures.*
*He leads me beside still waters. He restores my soul.*

PSALM 23:2–3

On a recent trip to Israel, I witnessed spring in full bloom. Hillsides that were brown and barren on my previous trips were now green and flourishing. Shepherds and sheep grazed peacefully in those newly lush fields, a beautiful visual of Psalm 23.

Seasons ebb and flow, and greenery in Israel comes and goes depending on weather conditions and altitude. A good shepherd—like Joseph, David, or Jesus—knows where to take the sheep in every season. When one field goes dry, He knows where another green pasture is. He faithfully leads His sheep to healthy places.

This is how He shepherds us as we shepherd others. He leads us to health so we can lead others to the same. What is true locationally in Israel is true spiritually with Jesus. He knows our seasons—the unfolding patterns of family life, ministry context, personal development, and life stage—and He is the Good Shepherd who sets a steady pace to the next healthy place. At least, He will if we *allow* Him.

If God led you to stillness, would you be still?

If He told you to lie down, would you?

Or would you feel guilty, lazy, or have the need to explain?

Maybe this is why David wrote, "He *makes* me lie down . . ." (Ps. 23:2).

From the first moment you set out to serve Jesus and His people, two types of gravity will relentlessly work against you.

The first is the gravity of the spiritual battle—therefore we compensate for negative flow.

The second is the gravity of an unsustainable pace.

Devotion does not equal depletion.

## A Passionate Plea for Less

The gravitational pull to overwork is intrinsic to ministry. When we love what we do and who we serve, it seems the more, the better. But as much as God commends excellence and hard work, He also commends rest and renewal. It's the rhythms that are important—how do we set a steady pace to sustain our race?

In my first twenty years, I willfully spread myself too thin. Later, arriving at my current church in midlife, the workflow gravitated in the same direction. But God put me under a forced restriction with physical weakness. I did not wish to return to my previously frantic pace, but I didn't really have a choice. I couldn't, though the work seemed to require it and often still does.

A decade later, the boundaries between a strong work ethic and a restful pace remain elusive, especially in crisis seasons. Balance is an imperfect science requiring daily evaluation and quick correction, like a man walking a tightrope. In pastoral ministry, you and your family are taking a long journey across a dangerous gorge. It is physically, emotionally, and spiritually demanding, and it requires careful balance and healthy patterns of expenditure and replenishment.

Over the years, my recalibrating prayer has been, "Jesus, do your work with less from me." As I drift toward overextension, this prayer often helps me regain sensitivity to the difference between *hard* work and *over*work. It's not so much about our less as it is about His more. Our more is always less, but our less is always more in Jesus' economy.

We overvalue our contribution and undervalue His, which fosters an unhealthy pace.

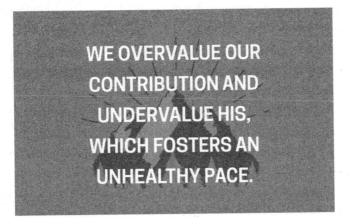

WE OVERVALUE OUR CONTRIBUTION AND UNDERVALUE HIS, WHICH FOSTERS AN UNHEALTHY PACE.

The first time I prayed this, it seemed God laughed. It was as if He said, *No problem, Captain Fumes! That's how I best operate—less of you, more of Me! I did create you to come up for air regularly.*

Well—duh! Did I think He would worry?

In His gentle rebuke, I felt divinely liberated from myself—free to limit work hours to an appropriate level of God-honoring effort paired with contented trust and consistent rest. It's a paradox. He calls us to operate from contentment in Him but also to cultivate healthy passion or ambition for His work and mission.

He compels us to hunger for *more* from the fullness of His *enough*.

As we seek this balance—or manage this tension—it's beautiful to watch God do more after He has convicted you to do less.

Practically speaking, the goal is a sustainable schedule, regular replenishment, and strategic breaks for deeper restoration. I'm thankful for a church family that sees my gravitational pull into overwork and admonishes me to moderate a healthy pace. They realize a healthy pastor is best for the health of the whole church.

Decreasing work addiction, increasing family relationships, and stewarding physical health have become a continued focus and steady commitment. I especially love when a younger family man in our church says to me, "Pastor, thank you for pacing yourself, resting properly, and caring for your marriage and family—it motivates me to do the same!" Our schedule unavoidably becomes our example.

Something tells me Jesus is pleased when His under-shepherds lead to health from health.

The outcome of a healthier pace has been good and fruitful. Less time forces clarity on valuable time and strategic priorities. Less human strain forces the admission that God is working and leading His church.

My friend Scott says, "This is Jesus' church, and He's doing a good job with it."

In all, a healthy pace provides an opportunity to trust God to do more with less and then to marvel at His work more than my accomplishments. The harder we work, the more we are tempted to seek validation and gratification in achievements rather than in obedience. God desires our deepest gratification and delight to be derived from what Jesus has done, not from what we can do.

God's capacity for productivity is astounding. Isn't that the understatement of all time!

Though He invites us into the work and mercifully uses us, He doesn't *need* us to execute for Him. Our involvement is all by the grace of God, as Paul told Timothy, "who saved us and called us to a holy calling, *not because of our works* but *because of his own purpose and grace*, which he gave us in Christ Jesus before the ages began" (2 Tim. 1:9). It wasn't my works that attracted God to consider me useful. My gifts do not enhance His abilities. He calls us by His grace and chooses to use the gifts He has given us.

Embracing a healthy pace begins with release—trusting Jesus as the Shepherd of both His church and our souls. Ask Him to do more with your less, then in clear conscience and as an obedient steward choose to operate at a balanced pace. Reliant sheep restfully walk at the speed of the shepherd, not of the other sheep. If you're an impatient sheep like me, you may need something like a shock collar.

### Better Productivity or Better Leader?

Does Jesus have permission to set your pace, or do you run to please others or yourself? Our Lord has entrusted us with valuable resources—physical, emotional, relational, spiritual, intellectual, material, and directional capacities—and He expects good stewardship of these marvelous gifts. They are the fuel of our lives and ministry, designed to flow in and back out with natural, life-giving rhythms.

*You* are ultimately God's resource given to His church (Eph. 4:11).

How are you caring for God's resource?

Recently, I enjoyed dinner with our ministry leadership team. Due to a construction fire in our school only weeks before opening, it had been a particularly intense season of recovery. It was a miracle story, too long to share here. Having followed God through the crisis together, our dinner was a time to come up for air.

These are exceptional servants of Jesus who also face the negative flow, fight fatigue, and wrestle through the complex challenges of raising young families in ministry. Mindful of these burdens, I tried to encourage them with this thought:

*A better you is more valuable than a more productive you.*

Say it in the first person:

*A better me is more valuable than a more productive me.*

While the two concepts are not mutually exclusive, the gospel reality is that our true value is in who Jesus makes us, not in what we do for Him.

Our *being* is far more significant than our *doing*, and our greatest gift to others is a Jesus-shaped heart, not a flaming pace of productivity.

What would happen if you brought a better you spiritually, emotionally, and physically to your family and ministry? As still waters and green pastures yield better, healthier sheep, God desires to shepherd a healthier you into His expressed love to others. He is more devoted to your maturity than your productivity, and He's more desirous to provide His sheep with good care through you than He is to complete more stuff on your project list.

It's quite liberating to release our death grip on progress and, like a child, grab ahold of His gentle hand to walk in love (Eph. 5:1).

The world and our inner drive tell us the path to a "better me" is achievement-based. This drives us with heavy pressure to lead overwrought lives, which inevitably leads to "worse me"—a less loving and less lovable version. When we, as dear children, follow Him and learn to walk in love, we become more loving and, frankly, more lovable.

Trading soul health for personal achievement is always a bad deal.

The program can be full, the schedule overflowing, and the task list never-ending—which it always will be—but if the shepherds are famished and floundering, the sheep won't be well. When we live stressed, we mismanage God's resources for His people. We rob ourselves and those we are sent to love. We prevent God's will at the most fundamental level.

We may get more done, but it will absolutely be less by God's standard.

If we operate from distressful places, we will not lead others to restful places. Frazzled pastors do not cultivate flourishing sheep.

Good shepherds do not drive themselves or their sheep at anxiety-inducing paces.

Church health begins with personal health, which starts with the leader. And godly leaders value and never stop pursuing a healthy pace—their own, their family's, and their team's.

This kind of careful stewardship is not narcissistic or selfish, and it is not for sheer pleasure or self-gratification. It is never exploitative. On the contrary, leading from a steady pace and fullness flows from God-fearing motivation. The life of Jesus within us calls forth humility and restraint, which results in a wise, sustainable lifestyle. It's not asking, "What is best for me?" but rather, "How can I sustainably restore and expend for the best of those I love?"

When Jesus said, "Whoever believes in me, as the Scripture has said, 'Out of his heart will flow rivers of living water'" (John 7:38), He was speaking of His Spirit as an ever-flowing supply of strength and life—first to us, then through us. He was implying regular renewal.

What good are resources unless we pause to consume them? Picture a marathon runner bypassing all the water stations along the way, collapsing from dehydration before the finish line. Better yet, picture a military medic who is too sick from self-neglect to rescue the wounded on the field of battle.

We cannot distribute to others what we do not possess. Yes, He supplies the flow of strength, but soul care requires us to pause and partake. Jesus exemplified this often in His earthly ministry (Matt. 14:13; Mark 1:35; 6:31; 6:46; Luke 5:16).

Those we serve are worthy of our devotion to disciplined renewal.

If you love others well, you will care for your soul in a way that allows you to continue caring for them for the long term. An unsustainable pace is quite an unloving lifestyle.

Bringing better selves to others' care is not only consistent with the gospel, but it lends credibility to the message of grace we preach. If we truly believe the gospel is good news—Jesus has done the work, our relationships with God are not performative, and He is a Good Shepherd—then we must display this belief in visible realities. God's people will hear us talking up "good news" but see us living out bad habits—our message will be incoherent and counterproductive.

Habits like building safe margins, guarding rest, taking consistent days off, and scheduling periodic breaks are aligned with everything we *say* we believe about the gospel. When we speak God's good news with our words but denigrate it with an exhausting and obsessive pace, we hurt the message we seek to advance.

A restful soul, measured pace, and gentle spirit are evidence that Jesus' gospel is true and that it is graciously transforming us. Grace is validated, Jesus is magnified, and God's sheep flourish when their under-shepherds operate with a passionate but sustainable pace.

## When We Work Against Ourselves

The "more is less and less is more" paradox is a biblical, supernatural principle.

The prophet Haggai wrote to spiritually off-mission but hard-working people. They were spiritually lethargic and apathetic but also malcontented on every other level—passionless for God, but passionate for their own stuff. Their operative principle was "more for themselves, less for God," which equaled less for themselves.

God commissioned them to rebuild His temple in post-exile Jerusalem, but the people halted construction for years because of opposition and hardship. As a result, God sent Haggai to compassionately but confrontationally expose how the people were sabotaging themselves.

They were off mission but working tirelessly to survive and sustain themselves materially. They rationalized that they couldn't construct the temple saying, ". . . the time has not yet come to rebuild the house of the LORD" (Hag. 1:2). God took issue with their procrastination because He had commanded them to rebuild. He exposed their misplaced and disobedient priorities:

> Now, therefore, thus says the LORD of hosts: Consider your ways. You have sown much, and harvested little. You eat, but you never have enough; you drink, but you never have your fill. You clothe yourselves, but no one is warm. And he who earns wages does so to put them into a bag with holes. Thus says the LORD of hosts: Consider your ways. . . . You looked for much, and behold, it came to little. And when you brought it home, I blew it away. . . . (Hag. 1:5–7, 9).

Though they were working hard, they were losing ground. They were dishonoring God and spinning their wheels in their self-inflicted sludge. Their work was for naught. No matter how much they produced or earned, God was lovingly ensuring it was *never* enough. They needed Him, and as they resisted Him, He was getting their attention by restraining their progress.

The people responded well to Haggai's admonition. They quickly repented and resumed God's assignment. Their enthusiastic response released God's resources in supernatural abundance. As they ordered their lives by God's priorities, His miraculous provision flowed.

Could it be that we are unwittingly working against God and therefore ourselves and our churches? Do we put hard-earned wages into a bag with holes? Do we sow much but harvest little, eating and drinking but never full? Like a child puffing at a dandelion, does God blow away our labor because we are chasing something other than Jesus? Are we hungry for something other than fullness in Him and obedience to Him?

Let us consider our ways.

When we make an idol of good work, we stand in God's way. We resist Him by trying to serve Him on our performative terms, and then He stands in our way until we come to our senses.

Living within our limits and by His priorities gives way to the unlimited activity of God.

He's not waiting for us to do more; He's waiting for us to get out of His way.

When we usurp God's design, He ensures that we lose. More becomes less. We need to surrender to His "less is more" principle. Doing so will transform our experience of life and ministry for the better.

Limits are liberating. Just as God was gracious to disrupt the hamster-wheel struggle of ancient Israel through the message of Haggai, so His grace delivers us from ourselves and from a self-imposed, breakneck pace.

### Assessment and Adjustment

God enables us to take responsibility for vital life adjustments—to consider our ways and realign our pace of expenditure and renewal.

Psychologist and author Martin Seligman wrote of the concept of "learned helplessness," a behavioral principle in which people accept and remain passive in negative situations despite their clear ability to change them.[1]

It's possible to convince ourselves that we are stuck—victims of our circumstances and powerless to change. A perpetual victim mentality is deceptive and destructive. God made us decisional beings and gave us the courage to implement healthy changes. Faithful shepherds commit to a kind of self-stewardship that enables them to care for God's sheep better and longer.

As we get into His slipstream, we expend and renew resources as needed. We work hard, expend well, serve joyfully, and then wisely cease our efforts and know that Jesus continues to work. He handles things well when we're replenishing from His stream of living water. He moves things forward when we're restoring our souls in His pasture.

*He's working when we are not.*

Pause to evaluate and adjust:

- What is the state of your physical, emotional, and spiritual life?
- Are you caring well for God's resources?
- If not, what adjustments or mid-course corrections need to be implemented?

For Dana and me, these evaluations and adjustments happen regularly—several times each week, then monthly or seasonally, and annually as we plan our year. We've never arrived at a static rhythm or utopian synchronization—it doesn't exist. Ministry dynamics are fluid, and the weekly schedule is unpredictable, which means time off for renewal is also fluid. If we miss a day off, we make it up. If we enter a nonstop crisis season, we take a longer break to recover afterward. We committed to a value that restrains overwork or depletion from becoming a new normal.

Fortunately, we're surrounded by church leaders who understand and have granted us healthy flexibility. They get it, and their wisdom makes them the world's greatest support team for a pastor. I wish every pastor was surrounded with such friends and leaders. As a result of these values, our ministry culture has become one of resilience and flexibility.

When our kids were growing up, Dana and I paused every week to look back and look ahead, asking hard questions. How did we do body, mind, soul, spirit, and family last week? For me the questions involved: Did I husband well last week? Did I father well last week? Did I meet the needs of family and soul? How does God want me to adjust this week?

These regular assessments and adjustments became our lifeblood for home health. With weekly evaluation and simple correction, you're never more than seven days off course, which is usually recoverable in the next seven days.[2] Transparently, our conversations were sometimes difficult and tense. I have never enjoyed hearing where I am missing the mark, but I've always savored the fruit of repentance and course correction.

In those hard conversations, growth and maturity required honesty, humility, and decisional courage. The needed change was not usually easy to see or receive. It was often more challenging to implement because of life forces working against us. Swimming upstream can be wearisome. Not everybody rejoices when their agendas rank lower than our commitments to Jesus and family.

Courageous love causes us to swallow pride, set aside fear, and embrace choices that please God. Pleasing Jesus makes displeasing others necessary at times. As the popular leadership and life-management author Stephen Covey wrote, "It's easy to say 'no!' when there's a deeper 'yes!' burning inside."[3]

## Seeking Balance, Moving Forward

Maintaining a sustainable pace will impact everything else. We multiply what we are, and our ministry culture takes on our example. Healthy leaders usually lead healthy teams and church families, and vice versa. When we allow Jesus to shepherd our souls to green pastures, we set the stage to lead others there.

We will give an account as leaders for both the pace we live and the pace we expect.

Driven and overextended leaders produce toxic cultures where others are also spread too thin. This is not only a poor example of trust, rest, and contentment, but it also takes the difficult stresses of ministry and unnecessarily multiplies them. This downward spiral generates a culture where the pastor is stressed and everybody else is too. Low morale and collective burnout will eventually materialize.

Relational and organizational decline may not be visible for a long time, but like termites, it slowly erodes souls from the inside out.

Balance is a dynamic, elusive target. As soon as you find it, you lose it and start addressing it all over again. A tightrope walker who survives is successful not because of perfect balance but because of acute attention to and quick correction of imbalance. Likewise, a good driver continually makes micro-adjustments to keep the vehicle on the road and moving in the right direction. Every day or week in ministry requires the same acute attention and quick adjustment. We never permanently resolve the challenge of pacesetting, but we win by devoting weekly attention to *assessment* and *adjustment*. Never stop aiming for a sustainable pace.

Account for context, life stage, age, family needs, and season. There is no one-size-fits-all approach. But in principle, it is honoring God to lead yourself to health for the sake of leading others there. He is pleased when we experience wellness and when we encourage others to do the same.

Given your unique context—how fast is fast enough but not too fast? My best advice is don't trust yourself and don't try to hack God's software design. Seek the wisdom of Jesus, accept His limits, and listen to those who desire God's best for you. If you're running too fast or slow, they will lovingly warn you. Receive their wisdom and take decisive, corrective action.

Remember:

*A better you is more valuable to others than a more productive you.*

*God isn't waiting for you to do more; He's waiting for you to get out of His way.*

Nurturing Practice #2 is *maintain a sustainable pace.*

What does it look like to holistically *apply* and *obey* Jesus in the stewardship of our spiritual, emotional, and physical resources?

Let's press on to Nurturing Practice #3.

## CHAPTER EIGHT

# LISTEN CAREFULLY

## PURSUE BODY AND BRAIN WELLNESS

*He asked that he might die, saying, "It is enough; now, O LORD, take away my life, for I am no better than my fathers." And he lay down and slept under a broom tree. And behold, an angel touched him and said to him, "Arise and eat."*

1 KINGS 19:4–5

My wife and I can walk into Costco needing nothing and leave with $200 worth of stuff. Of course, in today's economy, that's a couple of gallons of milk. But still. Recently, we ventured down a Costco aisle when Dana suddenly gasped. My momentary panic was nullified when I saw that a children's bounce house had captivated her attention.

"This is awesome!" she exclaimed. I could see the wheels spinning in her Nana brain.

I temporarily killed the idea. "Come on, we don't need a bounce house."

She relented, but something in me knew I hadn't seen the last of that thing.

I summarily forgot about the bounce house, but she didn't. A week later, I returned home from work to hear what seemed to be the sound of a jet engine emanating from my basement. I found the space overtaken by—you guessed it—a bounce house.

Minutes later, the basement was alive with four exuberant grandchildren bouncing their brains out in delight, and I assure you, the joyful giggles of four airborne little kids outweighed the cost and inconvenience of the inflatable.

Something about that bounce house caught my attention. It's only useful when a powerful electric fan propels vast amounts of air through it. The moment it's unplugged, the house implodes like a collapsing tent. That's especially fun to watch when the grandkids are inside.

An unsustainable ministry culture—or life—is a lot like a bounce house. We think of ourselves as that nonstop electric fan. The forced air of our human exertion keeps everything propped up and looking good, but we discount or disregard the depletion and exhaustion the expenditure creates. The resulting fatigue and poor health are rationalized because of the beauty of the inflatable. We couldn't imagine allowing our lives or ministries to collapse without our effort.

Then we hit an avoidable wall. When personal neglect costs us our health or right minds, we become less useful in His hands. How can we ensure that our leadership flows from the living spring of fullness in Him and bypasses the collapse?

We only have time to scratch the surface, but I want to examine the complex interplay of brain health, physical health, and environmental/relational wellness. As we do, please understand my heart.

We can never rationalize or excuse sinful choices. Sin or destructive behavior is not the fault of brain chemicals or physical exhaustion. We are responsible for the ways we choose to honor or dishonor God, but spiritually rooted choices produce and perpetuate physical and emotional conditions.

This is key. The stresses particular to ministry, in light of God's spirit, soul, and body design (1 Thess. 5:23), produce unique challenges to manage. Let me share an example.

After remission from cancer, I asked my oncologist how to prevent cancer's relapse.

He said, "I can't say for sure, but your cancer was an immune system disease, so let's begin with not ticking off your immune system."

"How do I keep my immune system happy?"

His overarching answer was "Less stress."

Then he spoke more specifically. "Number one, get plenty of sleep. Your immunity restores while resting, so cheating on sleep invites death."

Point taken. Sleep happened to be where I most compromised. Never again.

"Number two," he said, "eat a balanced diet of nutrients."

*Gulp.*

"What about my love for donuts?" I asked.

He laughed and said, "I'm not saying go crazy. Just be reasonable."

*Whew! That was close. Can't imagine a happy life without donuts.*

"And number three, begin regular, moderate exercise. Start with ten minutes a day and increase from there." I was deficient in all three areas he addressed.

I would now add a fourth to his list: Cultivate healthy environments and relationships.

That day, God convicted and motivated me to manage life differently, given the nature of my typically stress-heavy vocation.

If you struggle for motivation to care for your personal health, consider the value of more years and greater effectiveness in loving people. Your increased physical energy, greater mental clarity, and more hopeful emotional outlook will overflow into much greater influence in the service of others. It's a kingdom consideration. The forthcoming knowledge will help you sustain a full heart from which others can continue to draw life-giving love.

## Listen to Your Body and Brain

The four primary needs mentioned above—*rest, nutrition, activity,* and *environments*—fundamentally influence our comprehensive well-being. Why mention them in a book on strength in ministry? If Satan successfully hits these primary targets, he initiates a slow, self-perpetuating decline that eventually can draw others into our danger zone and cause them to become collateral damage. In my years of service, the stories of destruction I've personally witnessed or encountered in ministry leadership and church culture are too numerous and painful to recall. Most of the leaders began with neglecting the strong core we studied in Part One *combined with* long neglect of physical and emotional wellness.

We become temptation's easiest prey when we are sinfully far from God in soul, mind, and body depletion. There are both spiritual and physiological reasons why we are weakened.

Spirit, soul, and body—while difficult to cleanly separate—work together, cooperatively, for steady strength. As Christians, we tend to isolate and spiritualize everything, which causes us to ignore God's given physiological dynamics (and instructions) that contribute to thriving and sustainability.

Comprehensive wellness requires us to listen carefully to our brains and bodies as they warn us of the impacts of negative flow. Physical symptoms like chest aches, racing heart or mind, sleeplessness, frequent sickness, persistent discouragement, unexpected weight gain or loss, lethargy, agitation, inflammation, inability to be still—these symptoms and more warn us that our bodies and brains are screaming for attention. Think of these as serious warning lights on your dashboard; ignoring them is risky, foolish, and dishonoring to God.

> ## WE BECOME TEMPTATION'S EASIEST PREY WHEN WE ARE SINFULLY FAR FROM GOD IN SOUL, MIND, AND BODY DEPLETION.

As spiritual caregivers, we would never advise those in our care to ignore the signs of approaching sin or spiritual danger. Then why is it that we often give little attention to the notifications of impending trouble in our mind, emotions, or physical health?

*Fueling* our God-given needs strengthens us at all levels, so take a moment to evaluate each of these factors in your present lifestyle:

**Need #1—Quality and Consistent Physical Rest.** Our bodies were designed for stillness as well as motion, rest as well as activity, meditation as well as achievement. We are only healthy to the degree that we honor God's created order.

*Your optimal self emerges after seven or more hours of sleep nightly.*[1] Medical research tells us this, but so does the rhythm of God's creation. Quality sleep is the primary way our bodies replenish their vital resources, and yet for spiritual leaders, sleep is often the first domino to fall in our physical decline. Good rest fuels core functions like the immune system, emotional balance, clear cognition, and energy reserves.

*God ordained one day of rest in every seven days.* In God's economy, six days of labor paired with a day of rest is more fruitful and productive than seven days of ceaseless labor. In reverence to God and respect for others, devote yourself to this rhythm. Your family and future self will thank you!

*God instituted longer periodic breaks.* He called ancient Hebrews to cease work and celebrate Him with festive feasts in Jerusalem. For instance, when Jesus was a child, His family would have ceased their labor for almost nine weeks each year—three weeks of feasts plus two weeks of travel for each. One of the feasts involved families camping in tents around the city for a full week of harvest celebration. What a fun Father we have!

While modern Christians aren't mandated to celebrate Jewish feasts, the principle of extended breaks, restoration, and celebration carries forward. God's design indicates His desire for us to sustain a steady pace, regular sleep, consistent time off, and strategic breaks. These ultimately selfless practices are not negotiable if we desire to honor God and serve well.

Have you ever met a person who takes pride in slow-paced self-destruction?

They say things like, "I haven't taken a vacation in ten years!" or "I never take a day off," as if it's a badge of honorable martyrdom. See this for what it is—poor stewardship, faithlessness, disobedience, and just bad shepherding. God's sheep deserve a healthier shepherd and a better example than that.

If you don't presently experience this three-pronged balance— adequate sleep, consistent time off, and periodic longer breaks— you're doing harm to your long-term mental, physical, and emotional health. Lead by example, have open conversations, and encourage others to set similar margins.

A wise mentor once encouraged me that time is more valuable than money. As a result, during our church budget process that year, I vulnerably asked our deacons to consider granting me and my wife more flex time in place of the pay raise they presented. After consideration, they enthusiastically provided both. This shift in life balance strengthened our marriage and made us better servants to our family and church.

The conversation later materialized into a well-researched sabbatical policy. After more than three decades, Dana and I recently shared six uninterrupted weeks as a gift from our church. This midlife honeymoon was one of the greatest blessings we've ever received, and the substantive break brought deep replenishing, renewed vision, and restored emotional margin and clarity.

Simply put, if you don't rest, eventually your body will force you to. And if you don't ask for help, others will naturally assume you are doing well.

**Need #2—A Nutritious Diet.** Confession: I love sweet stuff, but overdosing on bad foods makes me sluggish, sleepy, energy-deprived, emotionally low, and unhealthy in other ways. The art here is to monitor what we consume so our bodies receive appropriate nutrition to function optimally. What could be more foundational or motivating for ministry?

Some years ago, I began intentionally tracking and balancing calorie and nutrient consumption. I used a free app, started reading food labels, and tried to make thoughtful micro-decisions each day. What most surprised me was how small, relatively low-sacrifice choices could add up to radically improved overall health. The benefits included better mental clarity, consistent emotional balance, increased quality sleep, sustained weight management, and higher energy levels.

Quick improvements were surprisingly easy to attain with attention to small decisions. There's almost always a healthier, good-tasting option to everything we enjoy eating. The more I studied, the more options I discovered. There is much individual nuance here, so you will need to experiment to find the approach and options that work best for you. Simply be aware that what you eat is unavoidably impacting your mental, emotional, and physical capacities, and then discover the plan that your body most positively responds to.

**Need #3—Consistent Physical Activity.** Over ten years, I moved from almost no intentional exercise to enjoying consistent workouts. Take it from a non-fitness expert—this is an easy-to-achieve game changer. For years, I assumed fitness required more time and money than I cared to invest, and I didn't realize the simplicity and accessibility of this value. If someone like me can grow in this, you can too.

This simple principle reversed my thinking:

*Any* activity you can enjoy enough to keep doing is the best program for you, and any length of time you can consistently sustain is better than none.

Unless you love to exercise, forget complicated programs and expensive solutions. Start simple. Design your ideal. Find out what works for you and do it consistently. Any physical activity for any steady time (ten minutes or more) will reap almost immediate benefits. The change in blood flow will improve mood, increase energy, clear mental fog, and increase productivity.

I never *want* to exercise, but afterward I'm always glad I did.

You don't have to be a physical trainer to do a little research and design your own plan. My workouts began alone in my basement with affordable, used gear. Ten to fifteen minutes per day yielded immediate results. As motivation increased, my sessions grew to four to six moderate workouts weekly—a brisk walk or bike ride, twenty to forty minutes on an elliptical or treadmill, or forty minutes of weights and cardio. Moderate weight training builds muscle, burns fat, and boosts energy, while cardio improves heart strength and energy levels. Simply *walking* will burn calories, increase blood flow, provide mental clarity, and renew a sense of vitality. I vary the plan to avoid boredom, and I pair some workouts with tasks like answering emails or studying.

Decide you want to *be* well so you can *serve* well.

Start simply but play the long game. Don't measure results in days but in months, and realize the best results add up over years, not weeks.

**Need #4—Healthy Environments.** Are your environments and relationships healthy? Are they stressful or restful? Conflict-oriented or peaceful? Restorative or depleting? Since you're in the ministry, we know at least one of your primary environments is especially depleting emotionally, psychologically, and relationally.

Adverse environments and stressed relationships exact a significant toll on our wellness, working against us at invisible, chemical levels. God's design of cellular-level events is marvelous if we cooperate with it. Good things happen in your brain and body when you strategically commit to good rest, a nutritious diet, consistent activity, nurturing relationships, and healthy environments.

## Understanding the Power of a Healthy Brain

We are "fearfully and wonderfully made" (Ps. 139:14), and science validates our need to faithfully supply our four primary needs. Here's something that few spiritual leaders consider. Consistent habits and nurturing environments activate chemical responses in our brains that comprehensively regulate personal wellness. Poor habits and toxic environments conversely create chemical imbalances that induce decline.

God created our bodies and emotions to function optimally when our basic needs are steadily met. As this happens, we naturally experience the right balance of brain-regulated hormones. Of course, this precludes chronic or outlying conditions that impede our bodies' normal processes.

Amidst much medical and technical information available, author Simon Sinek summarizes these concepts well in his book *Leaders Eat Last*.[2] He explains five brain hormones that work together for health and well-being. The first four—endorphins, dopamine, serotonin, and oxytocin—we could call "the fabulous four."

**Endorphins**[3] relieve pain and stress and make you feel good. Endorphins release when you exercise, laugh, celebrate, or exert physical energy. Our bodies become conditioned to crave these good feelings. As God said, "A joyful heart is good medicine, but a crushed spirit dries up the bones" (Prov. 17:22).

**Dopamine**[4] creates a sense of pleasure and releases when you complete a desired accomplishment or eat satisfying foods. The quick release is gratifying and habit-forming, which makes hard work feel good and makes some behaviors addictive. The positive effects of dopamine, when managed well, are vital for health.

**Serotonin**[5] regulates moods or feelings, and it generates a sense of calm, confidence, and strength. Serotonin releases when you receive approval and security in personal relationships, and it is withheld in the absence of that nurture. Insufficient serotonin increases depression, anxiety, fear, sleeplessness, OCD, and a sense of despair. Sufficient serotonin sounds like a pastor's best friend, doesn't it?

**Oxytocin**[6]—"the love hormone"—releases during sexual activity or when you perform selfless acts of service to others. It boosts the immune system and generates strong, long-lasting feelings of love, friendship, and relational trust. Oxytocin increases when you listen to music or receive physical affection, and it produces a sense of strong community, safety, and social connection with family and friends. You read it right— appropriately receiving and giving hugs is physically healthy.

The fifth hormone stands in its own category.

**Cortisol**[7] is the body's primary stress chemical, somewhat opposite of the first four. It is released by your adrenal glands along with adrenaline in times of fear and distress. As a result of complex neurological reactions, these chemicals are influential in your body's responses to stress—causing elevated blood pressure, accelerated heart rate, bodily inflammation, and a surge of emergency energy.[8] Sustained release of these reactions sort of places your body on its own toxic energy drink. Cortisol release affects your metabolism, immune system, sleep cycles, and many other physical conditions.[9] A prolonged or perpetual state of stress responses can make you chronically anxious and unhealthy. An "always on" stress response is like a vehicle with an accelerator stuck to the floorboard—a physical crash is inevitable.

While this is a simplified perspective of a complex set of neurological and physiological reactions, there's an important takeaway.

What's intriguing is that poor health habits combined with stressful environments or toxic relationships increase harmful chemical imbalances and decrease healthy chemical balances. But flourishing environments and nurturing relationships combined with faithful health habits *decrease* unhealthy imbalance and increase healthy balance.

The quality of both our habits and our environments either fills our bloodstream with stress chemicals or with healthy hormones, each with its own predictable trajectory.

Stressed lives and starved needs are deeply rooted spiritual problems, but they are manifested with dangerous physical and emotional responses—from a suppressed immune system to an upset metabolism to increased aggression and diminished cognition. Chronic stress and neglected needs cause the body to shut down nonessential processes and remain in crisis mode. What God intended to be an involuntary, short-term crisis response becomes an overdriven, always-on cortisol pump. Predictably, this leads to a long road of personal decline, bad thinking, serious illnesses, and eventual burnout.

Quite literally, our sin of neglect makes us sick in soul and body. Our attention to the body, mind, and spirit that God gave us leads to the broad-based health of all three.

Isn't God's design marvelous? In truth, a biblical life is a healthy life.

Translated in simple terms: rest + movement + nutrition + happy places and nurturing relationships = comprehensive wellness.

## The Ministry Connection to Brain Health

Daily ministry stress naturally drags us down a stress-response rabbit hole of chronic overdrive. Negative flow puts us automatically in the red zone for imbalanced brain chemicals—excess stress wires us with persistent, unnatural agitation, irritability, and anxiety. We live amped up with worry and care.

Subtly and slowly, this unmanaged ministry stress changes us for the worse, and usually, everyone can see it but us. So now you have an excuse—it's not really you; it's the cortisol! I'm sure people will understand. (I can picture my wife's eye roll when I use that one.)

Seriously though, there's some truth to it. Much stress equals much chemical imbalance, further activating anxiety. Stress + sleeplessness + poor diet + inactivity = a toxic physical and hormonal cocktail designed to break us and harm those we love. We literally lose our right minds and exist in a mire of imbalance and emptiness. The negative flow fuels negative biology which fuels negative physiology.

Here's the good news. The toxic emotions we at times feel in leadership, though harmful if ignored, are only *feelings*. We need to address this spiritually, but that would also involve addressing it physiologically and emotionally. Proper biblical responses include stewarding physical and emotional health. We are stewards of the whole picture. Therefore, our responses should be comprehensive in approach.

Spiritual disciplines like reading the Bible or praying—though always vital and effective—are only part of the complete solution. Obeying the Bible (James 1:25) will cause us to make courageous adjustments to lifestyle and environments, which will yield greater wellness in spirit, soul, and body.

God displayed this operative principle when He responded to Elijah's depression-driven breakdown. While perhaps not prescriptive of all situations, it is noteworthy how God first ministered to and restored Elijah's physical depletion before He revived spiritual passion.

*Lie down and sleep, Elijah. Rise up and eat. Now lie down and sleep again and rise up and eat again.* After Elijah was physically renewed, God proceeded to reset his spiritual outlook for ministry (see 1 Kings 19).

Like Elijah, you may not be in as bad a spiritual place as emotions or depletion makes you feel. Paul and Jesus both experienced distressed emotions that were not sinful. Paul rested and restored. Jesus received divine, angelic ministry.

In a depleted state, the brain's frontal cortex—the center of reason and risk analysis—malfunctions, making temptation more powerful and rendering us "not in our right minds." The summary is in addition to spiritual considerations, you may also be cortisol-overdosed, adrenal fatigued, and fabulous-four deprived.

Things are never so dark as they appear to be when seen through the lens of our depleted emotions.

Addressing our primary needs puts chemicals back into balance, which returns right-mindedness. This gives us an accurate perspective and guarded view of our circumstances. We see things more clearly when viewing through a right, rested, spiritually framed mindset.

One takeaway is this: you may not actually want to quit ministry or do something foolish. Those despairing feelings or thoughts may be unduly influenced or shaped by physiological factors projecting a false sense of reality. Something as simple as a nap, a long walk, a retreat with your spouse, or a well-stewarded sabbatical may correct your skewed perspective and help you recover a renewed clarity and passion to minister.

How sad it would be to experience predictable, avoidable failure when we needed only to restore through extra sleep, better nutrients, more blood flow, and loving affection.

Why would we self-destruct or walk away if simple, strategic lifestyle adjustments could help to renew strength and return joy?

More importantly, why would we bring a toxic soul into environments and relationships where God desires to use us to nurture health and flourishing? With good management, we need not live with this dissonance and internal tension. This very internal discord only exacerbates our struggle.

I'm not trying to oversimplify complex hardships. Rather, I'm trying to speak to the possibility that previously ignored conditions may be altering our sense of reality and are therefore altering the ministry others should be receiving from us. Before we hit a wall, overreact, or knee-jerk into bad decisions, it's important that we be certain we are operating with well brains and bodies.

## Goodbye Bounce House

The bounce house has two redeeming attributes.

First, when it finally deflates, it gives you back much space. The margins it was consuming are wonderfully regained. Couldn't you use some extra square footage in your headspace?

Second, since it's mostly air, it can be easily folded up and put away. It's not as substantive, massive, or permanent as it appears to be. Imagine how transformational it would be to allow God to deflate the fragile and distraught parts of our lives permanently.

When we neglect our basic physical and emotional needs, four destructive things happen:

First, we overvalue self-effort.
Second, we devalue Jesus.
Third, we disesteem what others need from us.
And fourth, we drive ourselves to bad places.

We need to fold up the inflatable, reclaim the margins of our lives, and faithfully prioritize primary needs. This is Nurturing Practice #3—listen carefully to your body to *pursue comprehensive wellness.* This both honors God and provides for others.

Sleep well . . . Eat well . . . Move well . . . Be well . . .

Relate well . . . Love well . . . Lead well . . .

It's all intricately connected, for better or worse.

The "you" you maintain is the "you" you bring to serve others.

Next up: Nobody likes Sick-Me.

## CHAPTER NINE

# BRING IT HOME

## NURTURE HEALTHY RELATIONSHIPS

*Fathers, do not provoke your children to anger, but bring
them up in the discipline and instruction of the Lord.*

EPHESIANS 6:4

Captain Fumes has another name. Sick-Me.

While sick with cancer, I was grasping to help my elementary-age daughter process how the chemo and medications would change me. So, we invented "Sick-Me." We told Haylee, "Because Sick-Me doesn't feel well, he's irritable and confused and no fun. Mostly he sleeps a lot." She understood and began asking me, "Is Sick-Me here today?" Suffice it to say, none of us miss him.

We all have a version of Sick-Me—fatigued, stressed, and living without margins. Sick-Me wears stress and tension like Pig-Pen wears his dust cloud in the *Peanuts* cartoons.[1] His anxiety-etched face tells the story, forewarning everybody but himself. Sick-Me can't see his own face.

His presence generally induces tension in friends, family, and coworkers, and he can instantly suck the life and joy out of those he is supposed to breathe life into. He is chronically distracted, physically amped, sleeplessly tossed, and obsessively focused on problems. Sick-Me is so problematic that he can even *pray* anxiously.

To be able to see Sick-Me and his effects on others, I've come to rely on my wife's nudge or one of my kid's gentle (or not so gentle) confrontations.

"Hey, Dad, are you okay?"

Sick-Me is typically offended and defensive at such love, but he can be put down with Spirit-led humility and self-awareness. *I thought I was okay, but since you're asking, I probably need to recalibrate and restore.*

Have you ever considered what it's like to be married to, parented by, or shepherded by *you*? If you could step outside of yourself and walk in others' experience of you for a week, what would that experience be? Life-giving? Energizing? Well-loved? Encouraging? Or perhaps fearful, discouraging, tense, combative, and combustible?

Are they generally at rest or stressed in your presence?

Do you cultivate a culture of fear or of grace?

When you walk into a room, do people mostly breathe in your tension or your encouragement?

I've experienced both qualities in leaders, and sadly, I've been both. But I know who Jesus calls me to be and who I want to be, and I will never stop aiming for that goal.

As we venture forward, let's shift our focus. Rather than seek what *we want* from our family, we would be better served (and serve better) to ask, *What does my family need from me, and am I regularly giving it?*

## Ministry Stress Impacts the Whole Family

As you cultivate the strong core we studied in Part One and then implement the first three nurturing practices of soul health, you will bring wellness home to your family every day. You will have the capacity to give what they need—which is life-giving to them as well as you. It flows in both directions.

The higher up the flow chart you grow as a leader, the fewer people there are who have awareness of your daily stress level and work intensity. The immersive nature of ministry easily and often results in long seasons of eighteen-hour days, in which case it's not only *you* paying the price, it's also your family.

Let's consider how the stress dynamics influence our families. My friend Dr. Jonathan Hoover shared some of the following observations with me in personal conversations. He graciously gave me permission to share what he is in the process of more deeply developing into a book on the subject of stress and burnout.[2]

Not all stress is bad. Good stress is like muscle activity that prevents atrophy—called "eustress." We could say your family needs a good-stressed you—hard-working, productive, and providing. But poorly managed stress becomes *distress*—too much for too long is always destructive.

An athlete lifting enough weight in an appropriate time frame will build muscle and increase capacity. This is eustress. But lifting too much weight too quickly will damage muscle—distress. The difference between eustress and distress is usually as simple as implementing a better strategy—readjusting the approach.

Maybe the athlete should lift less weight all at once, do fewer reps, lift with a different technique, or spread out the weight or workout time differently. For instance, I should not try to lift five thousand pounds right now, but I could lift five thousand pounds incrementally over the next week.

Likewise, a pastor can carry too much weight for too long, damaging himself and his family. But the answer is not necessarily to stop lifting. The answer is to *manage* the weight differently—to assess and creatively adjust. Implementing a different strategy that better fits your needs and your family's needs can make all the difference.

What your family most needs is a better you—a you that is managing stress and fatigue well and bringing your A-game home. It's not stress or fatigue that is the enemy, but unmanaged stress or unmonitored fatigue that eats up all your margin.

The sports world has a term for healthy, well-managed improvement—"overreaching"—and it's how great athletes excel. They push themselves slightly beyond their ability. This is called "functional overreaching," and it is healthy because it breaks through barriers and increases capacity little by little. This measured overreach creates intentional, healthy fatigue followed by appropriate recovery. The beneficial cycle yields growth and improvement—a great picture of steady strength.

But there's a kind of overreach that pushes too far beyond the athlete's capacity. At first, the body will try and may even succeed at extreme overreach, but not for long and not without a heavy price. This is called "nonfunctional overreaching," and it is always destructive. Too much overreach causes the body to revolt and never return to its original capacity. Athletes who do this ruin their body's ability to continue in their sport.[3]

There's a big difference between *can* and *should*. God created us to strive but not to strain—to stretch ourselves but not to harm ourselves. The difference is in how we monitor and respond to stress levels. Nobody feels it more acutely or sees it more clearly than our families.

Because of the complexity of monitoring ministry stress and the passion we have for our call, pastors tend to drift into the red zone of stress more easily and undetected. We push too hard for too long until we crash—nonfunctional overreaching. We bury emotional drain, ignore relational needs, and keep pressing forward to be and do all that is expected of us. Then we come home and crash—or worse—explode. Instead of wellness, we bring toxicity home.

The problem isn't the stress, but that we don't monitor and manage it. We don't have gauges on our foreheads, and we dismiss the warnings of family or friends. We choose to be willfully unaware of how stress is changing our mood, attitude, and relatability. All the while our families are all too aware. They live with us!

Like a strained muscle being forced to lift too much weight, relationships at home begin to be strained and start to revolt. The people we love always pay a price for our unhealthy habits, and loving them should motivate us to respond to bad conditions.

You and your family can survive the pressures of ministry, but first, you have to take off the blinders. Team up, lead into the challenge, and get creative. Start asking these questions:

What is ministry stress doing to me and us?

How does ministry impact each family member?

Can we manage stress differently to maintain healthy relationships?

Sustainable strength requires substantial time and attention given to marriage and family. To neglect relationships at home in favor of doing ministry is to hurt both significantly. When our personal lives are suffering, we bring that struggle into everything else. Toxicity in one breeds toxicity in the whole. It is deceptive to think that our homes can struggle while our ministry can be healthy. That kind of separation is not possible in gospel ministry.

> ## TO NEGLECT RELATIONSHIPS AT HOME IN FAVOR OF DOING MINISTRY IS TO HURT BOTH SIGNIFICANTLY.

### Escaping the Tug-of-War for Something Better

The first seven years of our marriage and ministry became a standoff. We started young and launched audaciously into the excitement and stresses of a fast-growing ministry. It was a privilege, but it didn't take long for our new family to experience the real tensions of unmet expectations and ministry imbalance. It felt like every facet of life was pulling against all the others, and it *was*. But our perspective was youthfully naïve.

We viewed the tensions as oppositional instead of synergistic. To us, we had entered a complex tug-of-war—the win-lose battle of our lives. This was rooted in fear as we had witnessed severe moral failures and family destruction in formerly respected spiritual leaders.

As a result, we viewed each tension as a threat to the other— family versus ministry, ministry versus marriage, marriage versus kids, etc. This made our relationship often high-strung and easily agitated, and we carried those tense selves into every other environment and relationship. It was years before we accounted for the fear that was driving these emotions (2 Tim. 1:7; Rom. 8:15; and 1 John 4:18). In truth, we essentially were living out each role in *fear* of the other.

The fear caused us to overreact—to pull harder on our respective ends of the ropes. Dana was on her end pulling for marriage and family time. I was on my end pulling for ministry support and personal companionship. And as they grew, the kids grabbed their own ropes, demanding resources and attention and seemingly pulling against marriage and ministry.

The whole idea of war was a false perception. Dana was as committed to ministry as I was committed to family. The kids were only being kids. Nevertheless, the perception created emotional reactions that did not provide the utopian family life we had dreamed of. It felt like a free-for-all.

Eventually, we hit that wall.

I'll never forget this day. I came home for lunch. Two rambunctious little boys were down for naps. Dana was sitting on the couch in tears. It had been a tense season for our marriage because of the perceived tug-of-war. Both of us were needlessly exhausted in the struggle for balance.

The *eustress* had become *distress*, and we were bordering on nonfunctional overreach. Every warning light on the dashboard of our family was lit up bright red. I knew if something didn't change, we would not survive. We needed to step back and rethink this life we were building, and Jesus held me responsible for leading the effort (Eph. 5:23; 6:4).

God's Spirit convicted me. I was in ministry but damaging my family—which was dishonoring to the Savior I was trying to serve.

We had been stressed on the phone earlier that day, but when I walked into the house, God gave me a different set of eyes. I saw the distress *I was creating*, and it broke me. I was regretful and repentant. That's not the man I desired to be. We had finally reached a point where I was willing to love Jesus supremely by loving my family well—even if that meant resigning from ministry. Again, my thinking was polarized—either-or, win-lose—which was flawed from the outset. Nonetheless, my perspective shifted that day from *pulling* for my way to *leading* the right way.

I told Dana we would do whatever it took to restore the health of our home. I'm sure she was rightfully skeptical. I apologized and repented. She apologized as well. We forgave each other for our insensitivities and miscommunication, and we covenanted with Jesus to serve Him by first loving our family well, regardless of the cost. That moment changed everything about our future. By the way, a single paragraph makes it sound much simpler than it was. God was gracious to break through our tension and give us clarity in very complex emotions.

A day later I sat, nervous but confident, in the office of the pastor.

My belief was that I didn't have what the ministry required, so I offered my resignation. I asked to be considered for a different role—anything with less responsibility. I fully expected that my resignation would be accepted.

To my delight, as with Daniel (Dan. 1:9), God gave favor. Our pastor identified with the challenges and responded with compassion. His family was not much older, and it turned out we were learning the same life lessons in tandem. The resolution was not to *leave* ministry but rather to do things *differently*—to be granted the grace to restructure and realign. Within days, our lives were set on a much healthier trajectory. What began as a tug-of-war resolved and, to our surprise, revealed a different reality.

Have you ever bounced on a trampoline? Contrary to tug-of-war, tension is what makes it work. A trampoline is nothing more than an omnidirectional tug-of-war that's made peace with itself! The right amount of tension pulling in multiple directions holds it together in taut stability.

The difference between a tug-of-war and a trampoline is the intentionality and usefulness of the tension.

A tug-of-war is win-lose, but a trampoline is win-win. It's synergistic. The goal in tug-of-war is to win by breaking the tension to the point of failure. But with a trampoline, the point of the tension is bounce, buoyancy, resilience—support! It works *because* of the tension, and if you start popping springs and breaking ropes—you quickly repair them so everything doesn't collapse. The interconnectivity and interdependence of the tension is healthy by design.

Such are our lives in ministry. If we lose the tension between family, ministry, marriage, and personal life, we lose big. Everything is impacted because it's all interconnected and dependent upon mutually created tensions. It's not a tug-of-war—it's a trampoline. Each facet of life needs the other, and each is sustained in strength by the other.

Our families need our marriage, our marriage and family need a healthy church, and our church needs our strong marriage and family. It's all held secure and resilient by the tension between each. The right number of anchor points and the right amount of tension provides stability and sustainability. But too much or too little stress or too few anchor points become dangerous for the whole. It's all beautifully interconnected and mutually dependent.

The win for our family was to stop the tug-of-war and begin crafting tensional balance. We needed to team up strategically instead of operating in opposition. Rather than pulling on opposite ends of the ropes, we dropped the ropes and linked arms. We began to address all the anchor points in wisdom, in weekly assessment, and in regular correction and adjustment. As soon as I dropped my end of the rope, Dana dropped hers, and we met in unity to start managing all the tensions together. This approach was a game changer.

This event was just the first breakthrough of what became many seasons of reevaluation and recalibration.

Over the years, we've continued to navigate ministry stress— eustress and distress. But we do it together. In covenant love, we affirm ourselves "for the other" and our lifetime love is devoted unconditionally for the duration. From that solid ground, we stand together in the struggle, fighting for all the God-given priorities.

We fight together for the whole rather than fighting each other from opposite ends of the spectrum. This shift in perspective and togetherness has made all the difference for the duration of our years. We've never arrived at perfect, but we've always found companionship in the struggle and enjoyed many perfect moments. We stopped operating in fear and began believing the best about our shared hearts.

When one tension begins to overpower another, we feel it—usually in disappointment or distress. But rather than overreact, we assess. One of us has quiet needs, unmet expectations, or unresolved tension. When the instinctive reaction is frustration or anger—taking it out on each other—God's Spirit reminds us that these reactionary feelings are warning lights, not bomb blasts. Instead of reacting, we seek to respond. We see emotions as response-able, and we engage together in creative strategizing and resolving.

We explore our present challenges and experiences, and we take immediate corrective action. Week to week we carefully navigate our way forward, each believing in the best intentions of the other.

What used to be a fight between spouses became more like medical professionals giving care. We didn't really need to fight; we needed nurture. We needed to give love—essentially to become caregivers for each other and our whole family—attentively monitoring and responding to the stress points of our trampoline-like life.

As our marriage matured and our children grew, we not only became best of friends, we also became the greatest of allies in the war against distress, destructive habits, and depleting life pace.

Nobody reads the need-gauges in our family as well as Dana. And my greatest successes have been when I listened to her assessments and leaned into meeting family needs as a caregiving shepherd.

It's been a long time since our days of tug-of-war, but neither of us misses those late-night talks. Albeit imperfectly, we now enjoy the buoyancy created by the tension of all the God-given anchor points of our lives. Each works to cultivate the health of the whole.

We minister together much, retreat together often, rest and play together frequently, and family together a lot. We offset each other's stress consistently and effectively. We are a team—friends, lovers, companions, and co-laborers. The journey was worth every growth point and difficult conversation along the way.

Why share this story?

Because this is the experience of *every* ministry family. We either tug-of-war or trampoline. It's either a stressed standoff or a team triumph. It's up to you.

Perhaps the key is to realize that Jesus gives you permission to do things differently, and when you honor each other, you are serving

Him well. You're nobody's hostage. The gospel makes you free to follow and obey Jesus, and He wants you to care well for your family. It's easier to please Him than it is to please everybody else. And in the end, He's your true and faithful provider.

When reentering ministry in New England after my illness, this was the general value that Jesus pressed into my soul. *Cary, there's another way. Let Me do this differently and help you and your family be healthy. Fear not. Follow Me!*

You have permission to do things differently.

## How to Do Family Differently

Let me wrap up this chapter with some practical suggestions.

*Be Courageous and Willing to Say No*

Are you willing to say no to things you've been saying yes to? It's hard to say no when others want yes. The peer pressure of our culture is toward busyness and away from flourishing, so be prepared to feel the tension.

*Prioritize Family Before Everything but Jesus*

Keep secondary or nonessential opportunities in careful balance so as not to consume every spare moment or family night. A frenzied pace creates a frenzied family, and healthy relationships cannot flourish from frantic souls and restless lifestyles.

*Maximize Family Time and Relationships*

We don't just do marriage and parenting—we *like* each other. In the spirit of 1 Thessalonians 2:8, we are affectionately desirous of our kids. We decided to cherish our marriage and family and to pursue deep enjoyment with each other. Now that our kids have families of their own, we have no regrets over the investments we made into a million fun memories. Every stage brings different needs, so your personal plan will vary from season to season. Allow for fluidity and resilience, but never lose the value of these beautiful gifts of grace.

### Make Your Motives Clear to Your Kids

A healthy family is not merely a means to a ministry end. Our kids should not be made to feel like they are victims of our call or objects we use for personal or sacred agendas. Rather, they should feel truly beloved as the cherished treasures of our hearts.

### Seek to Cultivate Closeness and Nurture Heart Connection

Relationships are organic and dynamic—they are nurtured not accomplished, and they are always changing. You can't project-manage a relationship or mark it off as complete. You invest in it, enjoy it, and tend to it with focused time and attention.

We're not seeking to mandate behaviors or legislate a household. We're seeking to win hearts and lead them into the love of Jesus, and that only happens in the slow-paced safety of nurture. The Christian home is a greenhouse, not a machine shop.

### Family Balance Is Simply Math + Courage

We often try to live 48-hour lives in 24-hour days. Insanity! We don't need more time; we need to do good math on the time we've been given. We have every minute that God gives us to do everything that God desires for us to do.

Good math will lead to courage—the ability to say no to ten thousand things so we can say yes to the few valuable things. Put up boundaries and live within them and ask God for wisdom to live within the parameters of His will.

## Go Home and Create Gravity

We gravitate to our places of success, and we love what we invest in. The parts of our lives that are thriving naturally become where we want to spend our time and energy. This is a self-fulfilling prophecy because where we place our time and energy is what thrives.

When we experience validation in ministry and conflict at home, a destructive gravity pulls us out of balance. Contrary to *real* success, we work longer and harder for work approval while avoiding conflicts at home.

Yet, when we invest in thriving relationships at home, the gravitational pull reverses and draws us closer to marriage and family. We need to fuel the good gravity of life when it seems that every force in the universe tries to pull us apart.

———

The glass house of ministry is a gift of grace. It comes with many unique challenges—more than one short chapter can suffice. But we've explored the heart of the battle. Seek to be healthy *for* your family so you can be healthy *as* a family. Create well-managed, useful tension and good gravity. Nurture and win hearts rather than fights. Team up, strategize, and creatively resolve the distinct family tensions of ministry.

Nurturing Practice #4 is *nurture healthy relationships.*

*Who we are at home goes with us everywhere.*

Many pastors who would never cheat on their family are instead cheating their family. How tragic to give the world our best and our family our worst! I refuse to love Jesus' bride more than my own or to love the children of my mission field more than the ones God gave to me personally. I would never want my family to resent the church and abandon Jesus because of my failure to manage stress and to be a gentle, Christlike shepherd at home.

Drop the ropes, stop the tug-of-war, jump into the fray, and enjoy the trampoline-like resilience that gospel life brings to your family.

You do have permission from Jesus to do things differently for the health of your family.

*Different* just for the sake of it is vanity. But *different* for the sake of health?

That's gold!

## CHAPTER TEN

# TEAM UP

## OPEN UP TO REAL FRIENDS

*"No longer do I call you servants, for the servant does not know what his master is doing; but I have called you friends."*

JOHN 15:15

Nirmal (Nims) Purja is a Nepalese sherpa who has scaled the world's highest peaks in record time.

In 2017, Nims conceived of what he called "Project Possible," an attempt to summit the world's fourteen tallest peaks in less than seven months. Nobody had ever imagined this possibility, much less attempted it. Many thought Nims was crazy and viewed his plan as a death wish.

Although Nims and his team made history with their amazing, death-defying exploits, their journey was not without risks. He and his team nearly lost their lives on several occasions, one of which he describes in the documentary *14 Peaks: Nothing Is Impossible.*[1]

High-altitude climbing requires oxygen, without which climbers experience a condition called HACE—High Altitude Cerebral Edema.

At one point in their climb, Nims went off oxygen to give his supply to another climber. It wasn't long before he began to experience a severe and delusion-inducing episode of HACE. He struggled to find his way down the mountain in the dark for eleven hours—growing increasingly disoriented and endangered.

His team was too far in front of him to know of his trouble, and with every passing second, his condition worsened. He lost control of his physical movements and struggled for mental clarity.

He described the experience this way: "I don't have enough power. I don't have enough strength. I was helpless. I was scared, to be honest. I needed to get down the mountain quickly. It was a matter of life and death."[2]

In his delusion, Nims saw what he thought was a Yeti monster standing tall over him. It was another lost climber also experiencing HACE. The two barely escaped their ordeal.

Have you heard the parable of the lonely pastor who lost his sanity? Similar to Nims, it began with excess elevation. He made an exhausting climb up Mount Self, the highest peak in the spiritual wilderness. There he planted a flag with his name and posted a picture. He had reached the pinnacle of personal success, but he was alone.

He had not factored in that pastors are not designed for such high places. Inordinate elevation and dangerous isolation began to take a toll. Spiritual lungs are not equipped for such self-dependent altitudes. His team continued safe climbs together on mountains worth climbing, but the pastor self-isolated in his unrelenting solo ascent.

It wasn't long before the elevation and isolation began to take a toll. The pastor changed as his health diminished. Unsafe elevation and unnecessary isolation created soul deprivation, making the pastor anxious, angry, and resentful. Spiritual oxygen ran low, nutrition was scarce, and strength predictably waned, leaving his mind and heart in a self-absorbed state of decline.

*Why does no one understand my burdens?* he brooded.

In myopic delusion, he blamed his team and imagined himself the victim in a world of insensitive and thoughtless followers. He was blind to the irrationality of rejecting companionship and then claiming to be the victim of loneliness.

He grew bitter. Finally, he blamed God for forcing such a ruthless climb. He sat down breathless and stewing at the peak of his lonely precipice. He waited for a long time, anticipating that empathy would eventually arrive in some form. But he only grew more deprived.

*Why don't I have friends? Doesn't anybody care?* he bemoaned, hearing nothing but his own echoes from distant ridges.

In deep darkness, he took out his cellphone to scroll through social media. The glory of his achievements faded as he scrolled. The elevation, isolation, and deprivation led to hallucinations as others' posts provoked him to dissatisfaction and envy. As a heavy fog descended and the night grew colder, self-admiration devoured the pastor's last bits of sanity.

For mountain climbers and for spiritual leaders, there's only one cure for HACE—*descent.* "He must increase, but I must decrease" (John 3:30).

Descend or climb on toward eventual destruction—these are our two options. No pastor should ever leave a team behind and climb Mount Self. Even in healthy climbs, no spiritual leaders should traverse the soul-starving altitudes of gospel ministry without a team and a significant supply of backup oxygen. Yet, even with extreme HACE, the most self-deluded or isolated mind can go lower. With Nims, every step lower brought greater clarity and less delusion. Descent is humility. Descent is a consciousness that we serve under the Good Shepherd. Descent is elevating the One who deserves the glory.

Pastors who descend from Mount Self find the oxygen and resources to rejoin their friends in climbing mountains worth scaling as a team. They regain a realistic sense of self and restore deep, energizing joy in the presence of fellow climbers.

### Leaders Are Lonely Creatures

Spiritual leaders are typically lonely. Each year, I interact with hundreds of pastors, and the majority will quickly admit they have *no* close friends. This is more than tragic—it's dangerous. The presence of real, godly companionship profoundly enhances sustainability in ministry.

We need soul friends. True friends. These relationships are difficult to discover, but I marvel at how many times true friends have saved my life. If you are climbing alone and do not regularly experience the spiritual, emotional, and relational strength of faithful, authentic friendships, please sense the urgency in these words: this cannot continue if you desire to finish your course and experience the steady strength of Jesus.

He often imparts His strength and ministers His grace through the selfless love of human vessels called real friends.

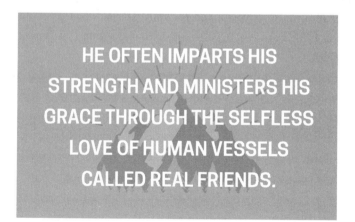

HE OFTEN IMPARTS HIS
STRENGTH AND MINISTERS HIS
GRACE THROUGH THE SELFLESS
LOVE OF HUMAN VESSELS
CALLED REAL FRIENDS.

What is it about gospel ministry that causes leaders to gravitate to isolated places? At least five enemies come against our growing real friendships: *awkwardness, fearfulness, busyness, grandiosity,* and *depletion.*

148

## Awkwardness

Awkwardness traces back to the unique dynamics of leadership. Because people find it hard to be themselves with a pastor and often don't want the pastor to be himself, our relational world can be saturated with insecurity. The gospel overcomes this, making us secure in Jesus and willing to be authentic and vulnerable. The truth of the gospel makes us so safe that we can laugh at our relational awkwardness or insecurities.

## Fearfulness

Fearfulness arises because of the risk factors intrinsic to authenticity. Will we be accepted or hurt? As much as we absorb human pain in ministry, can we bear the possibility of another personal hurt? Playing it safe seems wiser. It's easier to retreat than take risks, to isolate rather than open up. It's a psychological reflex of self-protection. In fear of being wounded, canceled, ghosted, or exploited *yet again*, we choose instead to withdraw and hibernate from hurt.

## Busyness

Busyness is an easy excuse. We bury ourselves in the incessant workflow, leaving no time for human connection. Regrettably, in many younger seasons of my ministry, the longing for deep friendship was there, but my schedule prevented it. Owning responsibility for this caused me to make some difficult choices. The midlife course correction has been relationally rich.

Often we reach out to friends for no other reason than to enjoy the gift of their presence—no other agenda. Whether catching up over the phone, enjoying a meal, or sharing a getaway, real friendships have proven to be lifesaving and soul-enriching. And what happens to the schedule when we take time to nurture friendships? It's still there, but the climb is easier.

*Grandiosity*

"Grandiosity" is the quality of being impressive and imposing in appearance or style, or having a sort of pretentious, pompous superiority.[3] An air of superiority ostracizes others. Paul wrote of these personalities this way: "And from those who seemed to be influential (what they were makes no difference to me; God shows no partiality)—those, I say, who seemed influential added nothing to me" (Gal. 2:6).

The self-inflated are empty, and their bluster is a bluff hiding deep insecurities. Inside each of us lives an insidious glory-hunger, which, if allowed, grows into a narrow sense of largeness (1 Sam. 15:17). This causes us to view people as objects to use and relationships as transactions to leverage.

This pride works against us. Arrogance repulses and repels, while humility magnetizes and attracts. John wrote of the isolating behavior of Diotrephes in 3 John 9. His proud, cold-hearted authoritarianism gave him a caricatured sense of dominion. He elevated himself beyond the point of relatability, so caught up in raw control that he unilaterally appointed himself to approve or cancel others at will. John called this out as evil.

The biblical preventative medicine is descent—being clothed with humility—by remaining relatable and little in your own sight (1 Peter 5:5–7). Grandiosity causes us to subordinate others, while humility leads us to elevate and cultivate others: "Not that we lord it over your faith, but we work with you for your joy, for you stand firm in your faith" (2 Cor. 1:24).

The *Wall Street Journal* profiled the life of Paul Newman and quoted him as being a man who tried very hard to distance himself from his onscreen characters. He did not like that his fans fawned over him for his acting. He said, "What people were clamoring for was not me. It was characters invented by writers. It was the wit and ability [of others]." The article went on to describe Newman as a man "weighed down by his own mythology."[4]

This is what undue elevation can do to a pastor who doesn't intentionally stay grounded with life-giving, calibrating human friendships. He becomes weighed down by his own mythology—the celebrity act overtakes the humble, grounded Christ follower. The leader begins to believe his own press as grandiosity grows.

The irony is that even when we are authentic (not performative or contrived) in public ministry, still the nature of a public platform naturally constructs an image that is at least partially surreal or caricatured. Real friends protect us from these dangerous, mythological selves.

## Depletion

Depletion is the fifth hindrance to close friendships. It's like not going to the gas station because you're afraid you'll run out of gas. In our emptiness, we isolate. This instinctive self-protection is a reflex that prevents us from receiving restorative grace from real friends. The kinds of friendships I'm describing would welcome your depletion like a warm-hearted host welcomes a weary traveler. These are the hearts you can literally crash into, collapsing in exhaustion on the front doorstep of their love and grace. They intuitively know how to welcome you, wrap you up, warm your soul, and replenish your strength.

Friends who protect us from the dangers of elevation and isolation are comfortable with our backstage selves—who we are most naturally. And likewise, we are comfortable with them in the same ways. Perhaps these are the people who are most acquainted with our weaknesses and insecurities, and on some level, they love us in them and because of them, not merely despite them.

Has God provided these kinds of friends in your journey?

Ask Him to.

An organic gift of God's grace, real friends cannot be manufactured. We could call someone and say, *Can we be forever friends?* but it won't go well. Developing these relationships does involve intentionality and availability, though. It requires devotion to time and attention. Often, those who petition God for godly friends find that prayer answered in unexpected ways. If you extend and expend your heart, Jesus will bring these friends to you in time. Though these friendships cannot be forced, they won't come through withdrawal and isolation.

## Cultivating Real Friendships

Over the years, I have encountered two kinds of friends. In his book *From Strength to Strength*, Arthur Brooks refers to these as "real friends" and "deal friends."[5] Deal friends are those of mutual convenience, and typically one or both sides of this friendship are based on personal gain. Someone is simply using you, or, God forbid, you are using them. Often, it's both.

These friendships are most painful when you believe them to be real but later discover it was only about the deal. The human heart can be devastated when the delusion is shattered by the casting off or cancelation that comes when you are no longer useful in the deal. The realization that you were merely objectified and exploited can cut deep, create disorientation, and cause you to isolate yourself from future friendships. This is a deadly and impoverishing response. You may avoid being hurt again, but isolation will hurt worse. You will also cheat your soul of many rich and blessed relationships.

Real friends are unconditional, mutually giving, and supportive. They don't cancel you, drop you, or speak hurtfully or untruthfully about you. They genuinely love you for who you are. They aren't trying to capitalize on you. They appreciate, encourage, and desire God's best for you. They rejoice when you are blessed, weep when you grieve, and walk with you on the mountain peaks and the valleys the same. They energize you by their very heart and soul and provide objective, selfless wisdom, insight, and advice from pure motives, desiring only God's greatest blessing in your life. They never compete or compare with you and can always celebrate God's goodness.

God uses the wisdom of real friends to give clarity in foggy, confusing, overwhelming, or emotionally complex seasons of life. Do you have friends who will tell you the truth even when it does not benefit them to do so? Do you have friends courageous enough to speak up when they see danger in your life? Do you have friends who are friends for more than the benefit they gain from you?

*Deal* friends quickly forget you when you are no longer useful. *Real* friends never could, and time only deepens the love you share.

The journey of writing this book has often been experiential. God providentially immersed me in the subject matter of each chapter—first hardship, now friendship. As this chapter unfolded, God permitted the writing to be enriched with unexpected relational connections.

Scheduled to teach a church leadership event in Phoenix, I felt impressed to route through Los Angeles to visit a friend of thirty-two years who is fighting cancer. The visit began with tears and a long embrace, then flowed to a slow evening of cherished memories, biblical wisdom, and talk of heaven. The doctors tell us my friend will see heaven's wonders within two years. We enjoyed two meals, read psalms, and shared expressions of our mutual love and appreciation. We asked Jesus to come soon. We wept and laughed and wept some more. And then we embraced one more time and said goodbye. This man is a real friend.

Early the following day, I sat at coffee with another friend. We had served as associate pastors together for twenty-two years, and now we had one hour together. The minutes burned quickly with mutual encouragement and appreciation. We thanked each other for the years of faithful friendship. We shared memories and dreamed about the future. It was pure, honest, real, and even a bit raw—two human hearts pouring grace, gratitude, admiration, and mutual esteem into each other.

As I looked into the eyes of my "big brother," I wanted to bless him, thank him, and express how much he had meant to me over the years. He wanted the same for me. Toward the end of our coffee, he smiled warmly and said, "We sure had a good ride, didn't we?"

I smiled and said, "We sure did, and I would do it all over again!"

Two hours later, I drove to LAX, thanking Jesus for *real* friends.

The week continued in more beautiful ways than I can fully describe.

New friends graciously poured into me at the development event. My hosts desired to bless me more than I could bless them.

God's next surprise was breakfast with a church planter in Tempe and his teammate, who had served with me in prior years. We toured the campus of their new property and mutually encouraged each other in the complex challenges of spiritual battle. An hour later, we hugged goodbye, took a photo to remember the moment, and again I thanked Jesus for *real* friends.

To my delight, two other longtime friends were available after my morning teaching obligations. By lunchtime, I stepped out of the hotel to hug a forty-three-year-old husband, father, and successful businessman who had grown through my youth group twenty-five years earlier. We jumped into the car and met another friend the same age who, during my first year of ministry, was in my fifth-grade class. He, too, served on my teams for over a decade. Overjoyed to see each other, we found our way to the closest In-N-Out Burger (my West Coast fast-food addiction), where we sat for nearly four hours reconnecting and mutually strengthening one another.

We cherished memories, grieved losses, celebrated blessings, and humored each other with therapeutic and encouraging stories and anecdotes. We laughed and marveled and admired and thanked. We glorified God over each other. The years of distance and disconnect had not weakened our real friendship and love. The hours passed like seconds, and finally, we embraced and promised to stay more connected, which we will.

These encounters are more beautiful and life-giving than words can express. They are the fruit of more than thirty years of authentic, relational cultivation. Real friends, not deal friends. While deal friends cast you off or cancel you, real friends cheer you on even in their absence, always eager for the next time your paths will meet.

## Expect, Extend, Expend

The gospel enables real friendships. Our standing in Jesus allows us to go at life with generous hearts—expecting less, extending grace, and expending love unconditionally. Real friends grow from seeds of grace planted in the soil of self-giving love.

The gospel frees us from *awkwardness* and insecurity, making us secure sheep in the Good Shepherd's care (John 10:27–30). In Jesus, we are fully accepted and secure. As we live in that security, we can take healthy relational risks. As we receive His supply of grace, we can give ourselves away freely.

The gospel frees us from *fearfulness* and risk, making us recipients of infinite love (1 John 4:18). Jesus never gives us a "spirit of fear" but a spirit of power, love, and a sound mind (2 Tim. 1:7). He enables us to love as He loves—lavishly, unconditionally, and perpetually.

The gospel liberates us from *busyness*, making slow, relational cultivation a priority (John 13:1–15). Imagine! The evening before His crucifixion, Jesus prioritized relational time to share a meal with his friends. He loved them, taught them, and washed their feet. At a time when He could have easily justified isolation, He chose companionship.

The gospel delivers us from *grandiosity* by grounding us in truth and love. Truth reminds us that apart from grace, we are nothing, and the love of Jesus on the cross declares that we are eternally valued by the heart of heaven. Humbled by mercy and valued in love, our sense of self is held in check by dual tensions of grace. We esteem others as better than ourselves, and all sense of comparison or competition is eradicated from our souls in view of the humility of Jesus (Phil. 2:1–11).

I marvel at Jesus' ability to expend more and need less. In His deity, Jesus needed nothing. In His humanity, He needed the same intrinsic things we need. He hungered, thirsted, grew tired, and felt deeply. Yet, He never engaged in human relationships from the point of need. He never entered a room seeking to receive but instead seeking to minister. In Matthew 20:28, Jesus expressed, "The Son of Man came not to be served but to serve." He came to people full enough to give and resilient enough to be non-reactionary to their responses.

This is how the gospel is the secret to real friendships.

We can expect less and extend more.

It's easier said than done, but it's what Jesus did. He expended Himself with abandon, even though everyone would soon abandon Him. He loved perfectly from purity. He loved lavishly from the infinite supply of His heart, needing nothing in return. In fact, His closest friends fell asleep when He could have most benefited from praying companions.

The more we anchor and immerse our hearts in His love, the more we experience it, and the more we can minister it to others. Imagine being spiritually capable of walking into every room to give love more than receive it, extend acceptance and affirmation rather than seek it. Imagine having such satisfaction and maturity in your intimacy with Jesus that you can overflow in unconditional blessing toward others, even when they only seek to use you.

I have yet to hit this target perfectly every time, but nonetheless, this is the highest goal of friendship.

As you open up, take risks, and expend yourself for others, expect some hurt but receive the healing and wholeness Jesus brings. The years will reveal real friends and deal friends, but love both equally and let

God handle the rest. Let the gospel inoculate your soul from bitterness or cynicism, and let it keep you open to your next real friend.

Choose to extend your heart despite the risk, like Jesus loved Judas. Decide you will be a real friend regardless of the risk of being exploited by a deal friend.

There's a counter side to this coin that's worth mentioning. Being *used* may mean that you are serving from the heart and that God has made you useful. Unless it is somehow abusive or toxic personally, you won't regret living in a way that blessed someone who exploited your service selfishly—like Jacob blessed Laban (Gen. 29–31). Sometimes those relationships mature and come back around, and the gospel shapes our hearts to welcome reconciliation when the time is right.

Patiently embrace friendless seasons and choose to wait restfully in the abundant friendship of Jesus. Companionship may be sparse or transitional in some seasons. You will face times when it seems darkness is your only friend, as the psalmist recounts in Psalm 88:18: "You have caused my beloved and my friend to shun me; my companions have become darkness." But in these times, Jesus calls us friends, and He will prove faithful and sufficient.

As He assured Paul in Acts 18:10, He will stand by you and lead you into real friendships in His time.

Finally, seek to build a team of co-laboring friends who will protect you from the dangers of climbing alone. Paul's most significant friendships were with his co-laborers, and whenever he was alone, he experienced personal lows. We've already seen his despair at Corinth in being separated. The renewal that came when Timothy and Silas arrived from Thessalonica cannot be overstated—his spirit revived, and his ministry flourished (Acts 18:1–10; 1 Thess. 3:1–10). His best and most fruitful days of ministry were still ahead.

God places the right people in our lives at the right time—life-giving, vision-sharing, faith-filled, spiritually mature influencers who minister to our souls. Team up with these gifts of grace, share the work, give away the credit, and do life and ministry in a team context. Retire the masks that ministry tempts you to wear and build friends with whom you can regularly release a long sigh and receive restoring grace.

Choose to pursue Nurturing Practice #5—*open up to real friends*. Mount Self is a lonely, delusional place. Avoid it at all costs.

But, to the contrary, there is a place quite different than elevation and isolation. It's a healthy place, a soul-restoring place called *solitude*.

No spiritual leader can find steady strength without regular visits to this place.

Journey with me into perhaps our most vital chapter.

## CHAPTER ELEVEN

# WORSHIP WELL

## ENJOY SOLITUDE WITH JESUS

*He restores my soul.*

PSALM 23:3

First-century BC Roman politician and philosopher Cicero wrote of a man named Damocles who aspired to the perks of leadership with little regard for the responsibilities and pressures that come with it.

The story hearkens back to around 400 BC, when the Greek tyrant Dionysius the First ruled over Sicily and southern Italy. Dionysius was young, powerful, cruel, and aggressive. He expanded and retained his power with great injustices that brought him both outrageous wealth as well as numerous vengeful enemies.[1]

Cicero described the tyrant as successful in business, ruthless in rule, extravagant in wealth, and miserable in person. As a result of his oppressive ways, he could trust no one and lived fearful and suspicious, essentially entrapping himself in the prison of his own ill-gotten success. He wouldn't trust a barber to shave him, a lover to sleep with him, or a listener to stand near him.

One day, a flatterer named Damocles was fawning over the ruler's lavish life of pleasure, wealth, and status. He surmised that no one could ever be happier than Dionysius must be. To this, the king offered to trade places with Damocles to permit him to taste the "good life" and to try out the king's good fortune. Damocles was delighted to accept.[2]

The king ordered Damocles to be laid upon a golden bed, waited on by a host of servants, and granted all the trappings and pleasures of a wealthy ruler. As this was set in place, Dionysius then commanded that a gleaming, razor-sharp sword be suspended directly above the head of Damocles and that it be hung by a single strand of hair from a horse's tail.

With the sword dangling precariously overhead, Damocles could no longer appreciate the beauty surrounding him or partake in the many delights that a king's wealth afforded. He couldn't eat the foods, savor the pleasures, or enjoy the privileges at his disposal—for his eyes were locked on the silver blade perched just above his head.

Finally, he begged the tyrant king to release him from the "happiness" he could no longer endure. The burden of the sword was far greater than the privileges of power, and it was more than he could bear.

Cicero wrote, "Does not Dionysius, then, seem to have declared there can be no happiness for one who is under constant apprehensions? . . . Yet, how desirous he was of friendship, though at the same time, he dreaded the treachery of friends."

The "sword of Damocles,"[3] as it is called today, is an oft-used metaphor for the looming sense of danger or constant pressure that leaders generally feel. This is also the origin of the phrase "hanging by a thread."[4]

Most spiritual leaders can readily identify with this story when considering the unceasing stresses of ministry. My pastor friend Mark once said it to me this way: "My brain is like a loop around a city with no off-ramp."

Eugene Peterson, reflecting on his pastorate at Christ Our King Presbyterian Church, said, "I can think of three times since I've been here when I was ready to leave."[5] During one such episode, on his way to comfort the family of a woman killed in a car accident, Peterson thought, "Lord, I can't do this. I don't want to be a pastor anymore. I just can't enter into that deep pain again. Or if I can, I don't want to. I just don't want to do this anymore."[6]

Must we live under Damocles' sword? Are there really no off-ramps in the endless anxiety loop? Does the spiritual leader's life inevitably lead to "I can't do this anymore"?

For many good reasons, the answer to each of these questions is no.

We belong to a Savior who stood between us and the tip of that sword. He took the blow. He bears the stresses. He defeated the foe, endured the anxiety, and bore the big burdens. As such, He calls us to lie down, to rest, to rise, to eat, to celebrate, and to restore. He *is* the off-ramp. Ultimately, the sword falls, but when it does, it falls on Him.

These truths must become more than well-rehearsed clichés.

We know these things, but we fail to experience them. It's all good theory. We can recite and teach it (and write it), but do we immerse ourselves in it? Do we enjoy it? In what ways and at what times does theory migrate from head to heart to become experiential intimacy with Jesus as a daily reality?

The answer is through *deliberate solitude.*

We learn to run to Him. Retreat in Him. We hide in Him as the only safe and sacred sanctuary of our souls. He is our ultimate refuge. Elton Trueblood, twentieth-century author and theologian, said it well: "A public man, though he is necessarily available at many times, must learn to hide. If he is always available, he is not worth enough when he is available."[7]

There is a difference between isolation and solitude. Isolation is a burnout response and leads to a sick soul, but spiritual solitude is a salve and healing agent to the soul, a spiritual immunity super-booster. Solitude with Jesus is a soul-energizing discipline that is essential to experiencing the gospel in personal and transformational ways. Solitude with Jesus is what makes our lives and ministry authentic—the public overflow of a personal, private relationship with the Lord.

## The Dangerous Path Away from Solitude

In large part, this book is about responding properly to the stresses and pressures dangling by a thread over our heads. When we live under the stress of that "sword," it is distracting and prevents the very relationship that most sustains us. Damocles' sword consumes our joy and devours the almost naïve delight we once had for Jesus and gospel ministry. It dominates our hearts with fear which drives emotional depletion, burnout, and unhealthy or sinful responses.

Oh, to return to and remain in that youthful naïveté that so hopefully and eagerly anticipated and drew us toward gospel ministry "as beloved children," Ephesians 5:1 says.

It is possible to go back to that place.

Solitude with Jesus is much more than a coping mechanism or survival technique—it is our very life and the most authentic expression of our truest self. We are never more centered in our identity than when we are alone with our Creator.

Researchers describe three typical steps to a leader's burnout:

Step one is depletion.
Step two is detachment.
Step three is dissatisfaction.[8]

When these three conditions converge in spiritual leaders, they make ministry intolerable.[9]

*Step One—Depletion*

This is that state of emotional and spiritual exhaustion that leaves us empty. Have you ever walked into a room of people, or stepped onto the platform to teach, only to feel that you have nothing left emotionally? That feeling is a warning light on our emotional dashboards. Unaddressed, it leads to step two.

*Step Two—Detachment*

As a survival mechanism, a depleted heart gravitates away from people. When strength wanes, we disengage. We choose to "care less" because we don't have the energy to care. The resulting withdrawal is risky, as it was with King David who detached by not going out with his men to battle. His decision to remain in Jerusalem led to idle time, temptation, and eventually his sin with Bathsheba (2 Sam. 11).

This disengagement brings strong feelings of self-condemnation. Exhaustion makes us very hard on ourselves: *I'm not useful to God. I'm not making any difference. I'm not good at this!* These powerful feelings eat us from the inside. Hard on ourselves and emotionally empty, we don't even have the capacity to believe those who try to infuse positive reinforcement. It's an emotional black hole.

This self-cynicism moves in two directions. When directed outward toward the role, disqualifying sin often becomes the self-medication of choice or perhaps is a subconscious form of proactive termination. We break ministry before it breaks us. But if cynicism is directed inwardly at ourselves, then suicide becomes a significant risk—as with Elijah (1 Kings 19:4).

*Step Three—Dissatisfaction*

This is the sense of being fruitless and ineffective, believing that we are accomplishing nothing in ministry. Not surprisingly, our sense of fulfillment plays a huge role in soul health and sustainability. The more you feel effective in your present ministry, the higher your tolerance for emotional expenditure.

The foundational question is: *Where will you turn to seek deep satisfaction?*

Highly satisfied leaders can sustain greater levels of depletion for a long time, but one major event can bottom out that sense of effectiveness quickly, revealing lethal gaps in the soul's health.

In other words, you can be busy, fruitful, and projecting the appearance of wellness while your soul is silently suffering undetected depletion. Surface fulfillment serves as a narcotic that temporarily numbs the pain and masks internal neglect.

But what happens the moment a sense of success tanks? Emotional and spiritual emptiness is exposed, and the future becomes unsustainable. Depletion combined with dissatisfaction will almost always drive us away from ministry. This is one of many reasons that the 2020 pandemic triggered a significant exodus out of ministry—the sudden lack of movement or activity revealed the cracks in the foundation—fragile sources of satisfaction and emaciated souls underneath. The path forward was unbearable for many.

In summary, high levels of negative flow are not mutually exclusive to high levels of personal fulfillment in ministry. Still, that personal satisfaction does not undo the negative impact underneath it.[10]

Consider the burnout progression from a biblical view.

*Depletion* is recoverable because emotional strength is renewable.

*Detachment* is a deceptive survival mechanism that should be viewed as a warning to renew soon.

*Dissatisfaction* is also deceptive. First, none of us can ever measure our true effectiveness from heaven's perspective. Second, our greater fulfillment is found in Jesus and the gospel more than in favorable circumstances.

Remember, obedience is success.

> **THE PRIMARY PREVENTION AGAINST BURNOUT IS NOT TRICKS OR STRATEGIES, BUT OUR PRIVATE WALK WITH JESUS.**

The primary prevention against burnout is not tricks or strategies, but our private walk with Jesus. He is our refuge, strong tower, life-giving water, and living bread. The soul that walks faithfully with Him will avoid depletion. The soul that is revitalized by Him will avoid depersonalization by living in the gospel reality of His affirmation and validation. Jesus calls us useful and makes us valuable. The soul that is fully satisfied in Him will abound with humble self-acceptance and deep spiritual fulfillment.

One way to view this is to consider whether our life orientation is more horizontal or vertical. Solitude with Jesus recalibrates our orientation vertically. If we are primarily horizontal—looking to others for fullness—we will always struggle to find enough strength. But looking up and orienting ourselves vertically allows us to receive what we most need from Jesus alone.

In this we "taste and see that the Lord is good" (Ps. 34:8) and know that "his steadfast love endures forever" (Ps. 107:1). We experience His abundant and eternal life as ultimately fulfilling (John 10:10).

Solitude with Jesus takes soul care in a vertical direction that avoids burnout and sustains strength.

## Why Solitude Is Essential for Pastors

Calling is a beautiful but dense reality. Being "called" raises the stakes for a spiritual leader, increasing the risk of burnout. Why? Simply because there is little to no separation between work and personal life. Like firefighters, medical professionals, or military personnel, we tend to embed our identities deeply into our sense of calling.

This sacred ideal pushes us harder—whether in martyrdom, stubbornness, or a sense of responsibility. We feel we must press through, go beyond human limits, and keep doing the impossible because, after all, "I'm called to this!" The calling seems to obligate us to over-extend and under-restore.

Our sense of calling obscures the distinction between our God-redeemed selves and our God-given assignments. The boundary lines of life roles are blurry. We begin to believe we *are* what we *do*. With no identifiable disconnect or separation, we live in an "always on" state—the call is the job is the life is the family is the identity. Therefore, depletion goes to our core, obscuring identity distinctions and making us feel trapped with no way out.

Experiencing personal fellowship with Jesus provides the only sufficient separation between our calling and identity—our true selves. Jesus provides the spiritual boundary and the clear demarcation between *who I am* and *what I do*. He is my highest calling, my strongest anchor, and my loving Lord. I'm never more fully myself than when I am alone with Him in quiet, restful solitude.

Only a right soul orientation—"looking to Jesus, the founder and perfecter of our faith" (Heb. 12:2)—provides spiritual differentiation, soul health, and strong stability.

## What Does Solitude with Jesus Look Like?

If I asked you to list five things that drain you, it wouldn't take fifteen seconds. But if I asked you to list the five things that restore you, could you? More importantly, does your calendar reflect their frequent recurrence in your life?

Solitude with Jesus is like bubble wrap for a soul that is being transported across rough terrain. The rougher the ride, the more bubble wrap you need. God taught me this lesson in three enduring ways in recent years.

First, during my early months at Emmanuel, many lonely winter mornings of moping turned into private hours with Jesus. He recalibrated and redirected my thoughts and attitudes through His Word. No human being could have done that inner work. He did it as I sat quietly, appropriating His Word and journaling my experiences in the light of His truth.

Second, during the pandemic shutdowns of 2020–21, I purchased a hybrid bike and began taking long rides on the rail trails of Connecticut. Earbuds in, worship music blaring, those rides became sacred journeys with Jesus along the Farmington River, journeys that restored my soul and recalibrated my heart in communion with Him.

Third, attempting to minister comfort to our church family, I began a daily ten-minute online devotion. We called it Enough for Today[11] and decided to slow-walk, verse by verse, through Psalms. The practice became so transformational for me that I would have continued even if no one else participated.

The Psalms are filled with the meditations of suffering people processing raw human emotions and experiences in the presence of God. They are the spiritual and emotional inside-out perspective of the characters and events we read about in biblical narratives. In the light of His truth, followers of God learned to differentiate between fact and feelings, and God preserved their private and sometimes raw meditations for us. As such, the Psalms are God's medicine chest for the human heart—unfolding every possible human experience or emotion in view of God's heart.

Since pastoring is a long walk through every kind of human emotion both personally and with others, the Psalms have helped me properly view, differentiate, and process the wide range of daily, often conflicting emotions.

As we love people, we grieve losses and celebrate triumphs of many kinds. How does a pastor navigate this emotional complexity? Even as I write, Dana and I recently celebrated our anniversary. But just before that joyful celebration, I sat grieving at the hospital bed of a sweet friend who was about to enter heaven. Yes, everybody experiences this kind of emotional convergence on some level periodically, but for spiritual leaders, the daily extremes are soul-numbing.

God's Word is the antidote. His Spirit renews our hearts. Isaiah 40:31 references waiting on the Lord to renew our strength. Jesus is the bubble wrap our souls need to be able to absorb the psychological whiplash of this rugged vocation.

Let me summarize six practices. Solitude with Jesus will lead us to *worship, commune, meditate, lament, calm,* and *connect*.

### Worship Passionately

When do you celebrate Jesus? Sundays? Maybe. But what about worshiping when the sermon, room temperature, absentees, music mix, and burnt-out light bulb are not on your mind?

Worship is a lifestyle of love for Jesus. In practice, worship is both when we bow in reverence or explode in celebration of our great Redeemer. It is when we throw ourselves with fresh awe and devotion into His mighty hands—when we personally experience Him the way we pray others will every Sunday.

In Nehemiah 7 and 8, God's people had worked hard to complete the wall around ancient Jerusalem, and Nehemiah assembled Israel to worship the Lord. As Ezra taught God's Word, hearts melted, souls softened, and God's people wept—grieving their sins and mourning their failures. Repentance.

God's response to His lamenting people is beautiful:

> Then he [Nehemiah] said to them, "Go your way. Eat the fat and drink sweet wine and send portions to anyone who has nothing ready, for this day is holy to our Lord. And do not be grieved, for *the joy of the LORD is your strength*." (Neh. 8:10)

In view of their failures, God's merciful strength flowed from His heart to His people as He called them to celebrate! This is what the psalmist refers to in Psalm 84:5, 7: "Blessed are those whose strength is in you. . . . They go from strength to strength." Authentic worship of Jesus is a very real source of joy and strength.

He calls us to experience His glory, knowing it will completely rewire our hearts.

"Glory" is a difficult word to wrap our brains around. We may think today of a champion glorying in victory. It takes many English words to describe the Hebrew concept of glory, but let's give it a try: dignity, beauty, wonder, excellence, majesty, praiseworthiness, holiness, and virtue. Glory is all the celebratory, delightful, invigorating, joy-inducing qualities of God. John told us that Jesus displayed this glory in magnetic and wonderful ways that enraptured and captivated those who knew Him (John 1:14).

Everything beautiful about life on planet Earth—everything admirable, enjoyable, and pleasurable—has its root, its inception, in the creative imagination of an infinitely beautiful and glorious God. He came and put on a human body so you could see, understand, and experience His glory. In solitude with Jesus, we remember and celebrate the reality that this *same glory* is active in our lives today.

### Commune Honestly

When do you talk to God? Psalm 62:8 teaches us to "pour out your heart before him; God is a refuge for us." We know about casting our cares upon Him (1 Peter 5:7), but when do we execute that in prayer? When do we dump it all onto Him? When do we give Jesus His problems back? Prayer is our moment-by-moment opportunity to sidestep the imaginary dangling sword and remember that Jesus bears the real vulnerabilities.

Several years ago, I was making a hospital visit with Dana. A nurse stepped into the room, and we began to chat. When I invited her to church, she paused with intrigue.

"You're a pastor?" she said.

As I affirmed, she continued, "I have a question for you!" Her punctuated Caribbean accent was beautiful.

When I nodded, she continued. "Who do you dump on?"

Her question gave me pause, so she clarified.

"Everybody dumps their problems on *you*. But who do *you* dump on?"

I smiled with understanding and then calmly pointed to my wife. Dana smiled, shrugged a little, and we all laughed. The reality is that I should have pointed *upward*. Jesus truly is the great absorber of our cares and fears.

### Meditate Faithfully

When do you consume God's Word? This is more than completing a reading plan or doing daily devotions. This is more like marinating our hearts in truth—immersing our minds in contemplating God's story and precepts. As Job said, "I have treasured the words of his mouth more than my portion of food" (Job 23:12).

## Lament Thoroughly

When do you grieve? God's Word empowers us to embrace hurt and authentically grieve loss without losing hope. Pastor John Piper said, "Occasionally, weep deeply over the life that you hoped would be. Grieve the losses. Feel the pain. Then wash your face, trust God, and embrace the life that He's given you."[12]

God's Word travels with us into the deepest, most brutal valleys of life—and it holds us together until we emerge victorious.

Sometimes the healthiest thing our souls can do is weep in the presence of God. Jeremiah wrote these words from the depths of lament:

> But this I call to mind, and therefore I have hope: The steadfast love of the LORD never ceases; his mercies never come to an end; they are new every morning; great is your faithfulness. . . . It is good that one should wait quietly for the salvation of the LORD. (Lam. 3:21–23, 26)

## Calm Quietly

When do you calm your heart in view of God's promises? The world is coming undone, but God's truth gives us context and blessed hope. His grand story is unfolding, and we know the triumphant ending—*He will be exalted.* Therefore, we can rest in hope. Psalm 46:10 says: "Be still, and know that I am God. I will be exalted among the nations, I will be exalted in the earth!" You are built for being still before His beauty.

## Connect Authentically

When do you connect in true community? It's one thing to *lead* the church, but another to *experience* Jesus in fellowship with His people. Do you ever get to be a sheep in the fold? Do you ever step off the platform and receive the nourishing realities of life in a healthy body? It's vital to do so, as the psalmist wrote, "I will give thanks to the LORD with my whole heart, in the company of the upright, in the congregation" (Ps. 111:1).

––––––

Research indicates that burnout in any vocation emerges when the stress outsizes the individual's emotional capacity to cope. Philosopher Richard Gunderman describes burnout as "the accumulation of hundreds or thousands of disappointments, each one hardly noticeable on its own."[13]

In my decades of service, I know of only one habit that consistently outsizes the stresses of the call. For us, it's Nurturing Practice #6—*enjoy solitude with Jesus*. Every moment with Him is the accumulation of a billion eternal blessings! So it comes to these two options: Do we gradually accumulate disappointment or consistently accumulate and celebrate glory?

As it turns out, the "sword" hanging over Dionysius' head eventually did fall and took his life in 367 BC. After seeing his own acclaimed play presented at an arts festival in Athens, he drank himself to sleep and never woke up. The most popular theory on his death was that he was poisoned by doctors working for his son, Dionysius the Younger, heir to his father's fortune.

In your case, the sword also fell. Jesus was there, and He won. He's alive, and if you listen, you will hear Him knocking at the door, desiring to share a meal and call you His own (Rev. 3:20).

Join Him. Behold His glory, and watch your stresses melt into His grace.

Schedule solitude and let Jesus restore your soul with His steady strength.

Open the door. Enjoy your Savior.

# LEAD A HEALTHY CULTURE

## 4 Focuses of a Life-Giving Ministry

*He will tend his flock like a shepherd; he will gather the lambs in his arms; he will carry them in his bosom, and gently lead those that are with young. Isaiah 40:11*

In the big picture, we're discovering three aspects of steady strength: *decisions for a strong core, practices for a flourishing soul,* and now *focuses of a life-giving culture.*

An easy way to remember it is: *core, customs,* and *culture.* In Part One, our *core* is the motivational and spiritual foundation that energizes us. In Part Two, our *customs* are the disciplines that renew us. Now in a brief Part Three, we will examine *culture*—the essence and impact of our spiritual environment. Think of culture as the air you breathe—both in and out.

Culture is something you consume and contribute to at the same time. It receives shepherding nurture and then provides life-giving strength like any healthy garden.

As the gospel reshapes us, it also reshapes those we lead, which becomes reciprocal. The leader's quality of soul profoundly influences the church body. When spiritual health is the norm, thriving souls become a gospel culture. In these closing pages we will examine four cultural priorities:

*#1—Teach the Word with Consistent Clarity*
*#2—Multiply Disciples in Gospel Mission*
*#3—Resist Elevation with Relatable Leadership*
*#4—Strengthen Hearts with Strong Care*

*Comfort, comfort my people, says your God.* Isaiah 40:1

## CHAPTER TWELVE

# LET IT GROW

## DEVELOP A GOSPEL-SHAPED CULTURE

*"I will set shepherds over them who will care for them,*
*and they shall fear no more, nor be dismayed."*

JEREMIAH 23:4

In Mark 6, just after the miraculous feeding of thousands, Jesus told His disciples to go to the boat and head home. He then went to a mountain alone to pray. When stitching together the story from three gospel accounts, an amazing series of events unfolds. The disciples enter the boat sometime in the early evening and proceed toward Capernaum just three miles away.

What should have been an easy journey soon became a stormy, life-threatening night of chaos. For at least eight hours, Jesus' disciples were lost in pitch-black, stormy disorientation. They progressed no more than four miles in all that time, with no way of knowing their location.

It wasn't until sometime after 4 a.m. that Jesus came to them in the storm, walking on the water. He called out to them, "Be of good cheer: it is I; be not afraid" (Mark 6:50 KJV). In John's account, as they received Him into the boat, the storm ceased and *immediately* they were at Capernaum, their desired destination.

Sometimes Jesus sends us into a storm to row in the dark for a long time. He calls us to obey Him, to exert and expend ourselves, even when our efforts seem to be accomplishing nothing but increased confusion, deeper exhaustion, and greater disorientation. Sometimes our obedience leads us to feelings of being lost and alone.

But our call to obey reminds us to keep rowing, even in the dark. Jesus knows where we are and enters our chaos. Then, at the right time, He stills the storm. And with a word or a thought, He can take us *immediately* to where He wants us to be—to His chosen destination. This is how He works.

All our efforts and strategies can leave us feeling lost in the dark, confused, and disoriented. This is especially difficult when we get into the stormy darkness by obeying Jesus. But when His commission is confusing, our assignment is no less valuable. He gives storm assignments just as He gives miracle-feeding assignments.

As pastors, we love to feed the multitudes, but we don't usually love rowing into the storms. We work hard to manufacture multitude-like results, but we also work hard to avoid sailing in the dark. But when following Jesus, He is present and working in both. In the first, we are cheered by the results—the miracle and the masses. But in the second, we are cheered in Him alone—His presence infuses joy into our chaotic darkness. He calls out, *Be of good cheer, it's Me!*

In this light, spiritual leadership is more about cheerfully getting out of Jesus' way than figuring out what to do next. We *let* the church grow rather than *make* it grow. We permit Jesus to do what He desires rather than planning His next move for Him. We let the gospel run free.

> **SPIRITUAL LEADERSHIP IS MORE ABOUT CHEERFULLY GETTING OUT OF JESUS' WAY THAN FIGURING OUT WHAT TO DO NEXT. WE *LET* THE CHURCH GROW RATHER THAN *MAKE* IT GROW.**

## 4 Focuses of a Life-Giving Ministry

On my journey, from the depths of weakness—weak me, weak church—God providentially led our family and church through somewhat of a reeducation program in gospel-centrality and true worship. He gently broke down our preconceived models of what church is supposed to be and materialized something even more biblical, organic, and beautiful.

He did unconventional things, always true to His Word, but grew them in unexpected ways. He led both me and our church back to health—physically, spiritually, and emotionally. He taught us to get out of the gospel's way and set it free.

Early in the journey, we stopped aiming at survival or growth or production and began aiming at comprehending the love of Jesus and loving Him in return. This cultivated a biblical culture—one thoroughly shaped by God's grace and saturated with energetic, overflowing worship. Visible metrics easily distract from the gospel-driven, love-based, organic movement of God. We celebrate God's fruit, but we also accept His greenhouse ways—His Spirit-led processes of growing His people. We seek to walk at His pace, grow in His grace, and cultivate the spiritually nutritious environment that permits steady, sustainable, renewable strength.

We have intentionally decided we will not run on fumes, and we will not drive God's sheep that way either. Rather, we will nurture a deep culture of restful, celebrative worship. We will lead lifestyles of genuine love for Jesus and let *Him* realize His desired fruit. I often say to our church family: "If we can't get there by loving Jesus, we don't want to get there any other way."

I'm blessed to say that I am a *partaker* of this environment as much as a *caretaker* of it.

In brief, these are the top four culture qualities He continually calls us to in simplicity:

## Culture Priority #1—Teach the Word with Consistent Clarity

Transformation always begins with teaching *truth*. How did the apostle Paul see radical life change in a short time in the pagan city of Thessalonica? He taught God's Word from a heart of love (1 Thess. 2). The *Word* did the *work* (v. 13).

The same is true in Corinth: "I was with you in weakness . . . my speech and my message were not in plausible words of wisdom, but in demonstration of the Spirit and of power, so that your faith might not rest in the wisdom of men but in the power of God" (1 Cor. 2:3–5).

A steady diet of God's Word, in sequence and context, given as He gave it, solves every problem a church can face and grows organic health among believers.

People care most about what they've been biblically taught to care about—therefore teaching the Word anchors hearts together in truth. It creates a culture of unity and mission. All the challenges of church leadership can be sufficiently addressed through engaging, biblical exposition.

The beauty of systematic exposition is that it lightens the burden of creative genius on the pastor. It lifts the sense that things are riding on the pastor's motivational speaking skills. The pressure is off when we trust the power of His Word over the pithiness of our delivery. Without careful communication of God's powerful Word, the pressure is immense to say something profound, funny, or brilliant—almost like a weekly TED talk.

Faithful ministry meets the needs of God's sheep by steady communication of what God says to them. It's not about what I want to say but rather what God has already said and how it makes a wonderful difference in our lives. Creativity is needed, but the Word is paramount.

Charles Spurgeon challenged younger pastors in this humorous quote:

There are brethren in the ministry whose speech is intolerable; either they dun you to death, or else they send you to sleep. No chloral can ever equal their discourse in sleep-giving properties. No human being, unless gifted with infinite patience, could long endure to listen to them, and nature does well to give the victim deliverance through sleep. I heard one say, the other day, that a certain preacher had no more gifts for the ministry than an oyster, and in my own judgment this was a slander on the oyster, for that worthy bivalve shows great discretion in his openings, and he also knows when to close. If some men were sentenced to hear their own sermons, it would be a righteous judgment upon them; but they would soon cry out with Cain, "My punishment is greater than I can bear."[1]

Our call is to communicate His Word as effectively, accurately, contextually, and applicably as possible—always seeking to grow as biblical communicators.

## Culture Priority #2—Multiply Disciples in Gospel Mission

Making the gospel a priority ensures that new believers are being born on a regular basis. Healthy churches always maintain an outward focus—ever communicating the good news and extending the opportunity for people to place faith in Jesus. Nothing breaks up fallow ground and tears down ancient idols faster than new life in an atrophied church.

When we arrived at Emmanuel, Jesus compelled a simple commitment before the church family. I determined to preach the gospel in every Sunday morning service—to both believers and unbelievers—and to extend an invitation for unbelievers to accept Jesus. This resulted in two things that wonderfully surprised us.

First, believers who had long stopped inviting anyone to church for fear of what political or tangential topic they would encounter began to resume their efforts to bring lost friends to hear the gospel. As a result, nearly every week someone received Jesus as Savior.

Second, the believers in the room fell in love with Jesus all over again. The gospel became not just the entry point of salvation but the river of grace that carries us forward every day. The gospel became the primary driver of both salvation and sanctification, which opened the floodgates to a fresh culture of grace and unconditional love in the church. Spiritual growth materialized organically and beautifully. The same gospel that saved us also reshaped and renewed us with a naturally forming culture of humility, unity, and mission (Phil. 1:27).

Of course, I took some criticism for this approach. Not everybody believes that repenting and receiving the gospel is as simple as Jesus said. But the overflowing joy of growing new believers is a powerful counternarrative to naysayers. It's hard to criticize louder than the evident fruit of God's Spirit.

Naturally, the birth of new believers gave way to a myriad of other ministry needs—from baptism services, to discipleship teams, to adult groups, to kids ministry, and care. But the fountainhead of it all is the faithful preaching of the gospel and discipling of new believers.

For everything we've examined about healthy pace, I feel an equal and opposite tension to stir you to press on in preaching the gospel. Don't be afraid to expend passionately and seize every gospel opportunity with devoted delight and optimistic energy. As we operate from the wellspring of deep contentment, we also need a healthy ambition to pursue our mission.

The gospel makes us both content and ambitious simultaneously—call it *contented ambition*. Our souls can be at rest in Him as our lives are energetically engaged and expended in the mission He gave us. Jesus was both restful and zealous (John 2:17) and Paul stated that he would "most gladly spend and be spent for your souls" (2 Cor. 12:15).

Early in the restoration of our church, God embedded three priorities in my weekly function—*feed, fellowship, follow up* (and repeat). Amidst the morass of problems that I couldn't fix, these were three disciplines I *could* do faithfully. Feed the sheep God's Word. Fellowship by building real relationships. Follow up in reaching and discipling new believers. Jesus left us on earth to be His church for this purpose. We exist to reach and build disciples through the message of His good news in cultures of grace.

If we continue to reset around the gospel, God will always be doing something eternal and special through our ministries. No matter how we feel or what hardships we're facing, we are always only one gospel presentation away from another potential miracle. A commitment to giving the gospel consistently, especially in a spiritually dark culture, will unavoidably bring people to Jesus.

There is no magic bullet for church growth—we let it grow by preaching the good news and tending to an organic, healthy greenhouse environment. We let the gospel run free and get out of its way. We stop preventing the moving of God's Spirit by lifting the bushels from our lights and holding them high once again.[2] The gospel of Jesus is the power of God to salvation (Rom. 1:16).

We are messengers, not manufacturers. We do not operate machine shops; we cultivate greenhouses. The former shapes identical objects by machines and sheer brute force. The latter protects and grows tender plants to maturity and fruitfulness in protected places. The former is a loud, destructive, mechanized process. The latter is a quiet, safe, nutrient-rich environment.

When we cultivate gospel-saturated environments, fruit will follow—at what rate or to what degree is God's to determine. We tend the greenhouse; He grows the fruit.

### Culture Priority #3— Resist Elevation with Relatable Leadership

If Jesus was anything, He was *relatable*. But pastors often find it difficult to drop their guard and be approachable. On the contrary, some intentionally foster a sense of superiority as we've discussed. Why?

Ministry makes an easy mistress. The natural gravity of the good hearts of God's people is to elevate (the Bible word is "esteem") their leader, and the natural gravity of the leader's flesh is the inordinate desire for admiration. Scripture profiles this many times over—from ancient Israel demanding a king to the Corinthians arguing over associations with Paul or Apollos.

When God's people make Jesus preeminent, they can extend appropriate esteem (1 Thess. 5:13; Heb. 13:7) without forgetting their pastor's humanity. And a spiritually grounded leader can appropriate that esteem wisely by stewarding influence and serving by example.

But when the leader's heart inordinately desires and fosters dominion (1 Peter 5:1–6) or cultivates a fear-based culture, things quickly go south.

Pastors aren't celebrities or authorities unto themselves; they are growing Christians called to be examples and to provide caring, spiritual oversight. They are to do so with a spirit of humility (v. 5), in submission to God's Word (v. 2), in teams (vv. 1, 5), and in accountable, exemplary ways (v. 3). It shouldn't be lost to us that this admonition was given by the aged and well-seasoned version of Jesus' most renegade, impetuous, and flagrant disciple—Peter.

We are a weak lot, and we make poor lords—and we know it. Biblical leadership refuses to see people as useful. It values relationships as the priority, and it cannot lead by man-centered fear tactics or intimidation. We lead by serving, not by bullying.

We *lead* sheep; we don't *drive* them. As much as the church needs us, the church also needs to be protected from us—at least from our flesh. The culture of our leadership should elevate Jesus in the eyes of His bride, realizing she belongs to Him and He deserves her purest and highest devotion.

When we selfishly and privately seek her allegiance, we cross into dangerous territory. Truly, in the heart of the bride, He must increase, and we must decrease (John 3:30).

Do you relish celebrity or cultivate an air of superiority? Does your demeanor ostracize people as being beneath you, or does it put them at ease as peers and highly esteemed friends?

In short, are you relatable?

The pathway of celebrity leadership and authoritarianism is strewn with self-destruction, battered sheep, and broken business-model churches. The slow and steady road of relational, relatable leadership is a good road—it's the Jesus road. The gradual cultivation of a meek and humble soul, a close-knit family, and a joyfully relational church family is a good work worthy of your life investment. The pastor committed to this long, steady walk with Jesus will be fruitful.

## Culture Priority #4—Strengthen Hearts with Strong Care

In his book *The Motive*, author Patrick Lencioni describes the dichotomy between what he calls "reward-centered leadership" versus "responsibility-centered leadership." Reward-centered leaders seek titles and perks but avoid the real responsibilities that servitude requires. Responsibility-centered leaders embrace service and care.[3]

Jesus expressed that He came not to be served but to serve and give His life (Matt. 20:28). Lencioni asks an insightful question (I'm adding the word "pastor" to my paraphrase):

Do I merely want to *be* a pastor? Or do I want to *do* what pastors *do*?[4]

Pastors *pastor*. We care for sheep. We love people. We bear burdens and absorb hurt and feel deeply without being defined by those feelings. We help emotional people know how to process and place those emotions. We enter hard, messy things so we can help anxious sheep be at rest, and we assist upset people in dealing biblically with their feelings. We take the high road to lead God's sheep to tender nurture.

We extend all the grace we've been given to the sheep that grow under our supervision.

We enter tactfully and tenderly into difficult conversations to make peace from the peace we have received.

I've known men who wanted to *be* a pastor. They sought prominence, platform, perceived power, or a set of perks. But they didn't want to *do* what pastors *do*. They didn't want the hard heart work of study, burden-bearing, soul-nurturing, and disciple-making. They disdained the sacrifice of service—accessibility, loss of privacy, fluidity of schedule, criticism, the pressure of answering to many people, and the general glass-house life. They wanted some imagined form of prestige or identity (however skewed or small) while repudiating the actual privilege of shepherding God's people.

Jesus called Himself the Good Shepherd. The very essence of pastoral ministry is cooperating with His care for His church. To the degree that we experience that care personally, we become conduits of it corporately. In a large sense, the leader's soul is contagious, and the church culture takes on the shape of the leader's heart for Jesus.

The beautiful reality is this: as we care for God's people, He will care for everything else.

I've heard pastors say, "There's just never enough money." I know what they mean, but the thought is an accusation against God. It's like thinking, *If only God would provide, we could get a lot more done for Him!*

God isn't dropping the ball or failing us. There may not always be money for my ideas or desires, but God always provides for His. The church that faithfully cares for Jesus' sheep will always have enough resources to do so. It's what He does.

It was wonderful when God dropped this realization into my heart: *Jesus has given me all the resources He wants me to have to do everything He wants me to do right now.* The pressure of fundraising evaporated, making me free to be a contented shepherd cultivating good health at God's pace of provision.

Pertaining to Isaiah 40:11 where God states that He will "gently lead those that are with young," Ray Ortlund once made a brilliant and insightful statement. He said, "If young moms can follow you cheerfully, you're doing it right."[5] The picture of burdened young mothers breathlessly, frantically, anxiously trying to keep up with an overaggressive, outpacing shepherd brought profound resolve to my heart.

If Jesus leads "those that are with young" *gently*, then so will I.

"'Woe to the shepherds who destroy and scatter the sheep of my pasture!' declares the LORD" in Jeremiah 23:1. It is often a hypocritical blind spot that those who deal harshly and greedily with God's people expect those same people to deal gently and generously with them. We all need gentle shepherding. Sow harshness, reap harshness; sow gentleness, reap gentleness. Sow generosity, reap generosity. But never forget—Jesus is gentle.

Cultivation and care is long, slow, tedious work. Fruit is sometimes decades in coming. Jesus has given a lifetime runway of sanctification in environments of infinite grace. What does He find in the sheepfold under your care? Division? Disunity? Contention? Malnourishment? Exhaustion? Frazzled families? Depleted staff? Competition? Comparison? Politics and power struggles?

This is often a reflection of a proud or neglectful shepherd.

Or does Jesus find well-fed, restful, peaceable, flourishing sheep who are well-cared for in grace and comfort? May we seek to have the heart of Isaiah: "The Lord God has given me the tongue of those who are taught, that I may know how to sustain with a word him who is weary" (Isa. 50:4). And the heart of Paul in 2 Timothy 2:24–25: "And the Lord's servant must not be quarrelsome but kind to everyone, able to teach, patiently enduring evil, correcting his opponents with gentleness. God may perhaps grant them repentance leading to a knowledge of the truth."

## Focus on Health Not Growth

The question pastors most often ask me begins this way, "How do I get people to . . . ?"

Regardless of the rest of the question, the foundational framework is flawed. Our questions should begin with "How do I *give* . . . ?" or "How do we *provide* . . . ?"

As we provide biblical care in a healthy culture, God's sheep grow, multiply, and give back naturally from sincere hearts of love. Jesus works from the inside out. Falling in love with Him overflows in willing lifestyles of love, service, generosity, and worship.

This organic fruitfulness is always more authentic and abundant than any behavior modification could temporarily inspire. The love of Jesus compels love for Jesus, which naturally flows outward from sustainable, renewable motives. The result is life-giving, healthy growth—real growth versus contrived, forced, manufactured, or artificial growth.

Because of this, focusing on growth is flawed, but focusing on health is fruitful.

All churches have problems, but healthy churches have fewer. When a body is declining, the stress factors rise exponentially. People are more restless, agitated, unsettled, and unhealthy. In these environments, more families are fragmenting, more marriages are failing, more Christians are quitting, and more people are gossiping or striving against one another.

But the counter is also true. In a grace-saturated, biblical culture, health is nurtured. Wholeness and healing are emphasized. Humility grows. Competition and comparison shrivel up and die. Judgmental postures and personal strivings fade away. Relational reconciliation and unity are valued in the light of gospel reconciliation.

Intentionally cultivating health is preventative and preservative—like vitamins building the immune system. Where hearts follow Jesus more authentically, drama decreases, trauma diminishes, anxiety settles, and God's church becomes a sanctuary—a safe refuge of green pasture and still waters.

We need to examine our shepherding. If people within our influence are not flourishing, that may reflect on the health we are bringing. Healthy souls make a healthy culture.

## A Long Walk in the Rain

Not long after arriving in New England, I became aware of some grim realities. The church facility and finances were in dire condition. Our monthly deficit exceeded $20,000. The building needed more than one million dollars' worth of work. In addition to this, my own family finances were in steep decline as the transition had resulted in significant loss.

My deep, dark pit was so overwhelming I couldn't see daylight.

Each Sunday morning, I would stand at the office window imagining that no cars would enter the parking lot that day. With each family that arrived, my heart leaped with a dash of hope. Sunday after Sunday, after concluding the morning message, I imagined nobody would come back.

Oh, the mind games Satan played.

Then there was the fateful moment when I discovered the monthly deficit and realized we were less than six months from total insolvency. The stark revelation hit like a ton of bricks. It was mid-fall. The clouds matched my soul. Into the evening, steady rain fell. To an ancient Israelite, this would have represented the favor of God in a dry and thirsty land, but to a pouty new pastor, this was liquid dreariness dousing the last remaining flickers of hope from the embers of my heart.

At about 9 p.m., I donned a rain jacket.

"Where are you going?" Dana asked.

"For a walk." My tone was flat.

"Right now? In this rain?" she protested.

"Yes, that's just how I feel." As I answered, I stepped into the night and began the long walk down the hill from our parsonage into the vast, crack-laden parking lot of our cavernous church. I walked a few miles in the rain that night. For the first half, I cried to God in confusion. I told Him this was too much.

An hour later, I returned to the dark parking lot. The lights had been inoperable for years. A thousand raindrops pelted my hood like a hoard of demon woodpeckers mocking me. The building itself cast a daunting shadow against the pale gray night as if to scream at me, *You shall not pass!*

It was like a warped version of a Lord of the Rings epic—surreal.

This may seem a bit overdramatized, but it's true to how I felt that night.

Then I did something almost embarrassing. I pointed to the broken building, looked up to the heavens, and shouted at God:

"God—that building is Yours. This church is Yours. This school is Yours. These people are Yours. And if You plan to save it, You'd better do it soon! I don't have a plan for this level of impossibility. This is *Your* problem, and I yield. I'll preach the gospel and call others to prayer. I'll love Your people. I'll pour myself into new disciples. But You must do something beyond us."

My tone was desperate and cynical. My attitude held a few bits of faith mixed in with heaping mounds of doubt. My fear and self-cynicism were abundant.

Then I said one more thing.

"God, if this is You breaking me a second time after cancer—if this is You bringing me here to ride over this cliff into insolvency with this church, to bear the blame for the failure—then I surrender. If I'm Noah and I preach, and nobody joins me on the ark, if I'm Jeremiah and nobody heeds my warnings, or if I'm Ezekiel and this is my riverbank in Babylon—*I yield*!

"Behold the servant of Jesus. Be it unto me according to your word" (paraphrase of Luke 1:38).

I let it go.

And little did I realize, in so doing, I was also letting it grow.

Perhaps He is calling you to the same decision.

Cultivate health. Put growth back in Jesus' hands.

This is the arrangement most conducive to steady strength.

*I will go in the strength of the Lord God.* Psalm 71:16 KJV

# TAKE THE LONG VIEW

*Though ye have lien among the pots, yet shall ye be as the wings of a dove covered with silver, and her feathers with yellow gold.*

PSALM 68:13 KJV

We started our journey by talking about wounded wings—afraid to fly again.

I hope these chapters have given you a reset and renewed hope that you can still fly.

Psalm 68 speaks about wings. Throughout the entire psalm, David contrasts both mighty and weak people in relation to God—power flees from Him, but weakness is exalted with Him. It's reminiscent of Isaiah 40:31, waiting on God for renewed strength; and 2 Corinthians 12:9, His strength is perfected in our weakness.

In this psalm, Jesus is a mighty, conquering hero with a gentle shepherd's heart. In one moment, He vanquishes powerful enemies, but the next, He is lavishly good to the poor and vulnerable. He brings down blustering big shots and lifts the little guys. Kings and armies flee before Him as He elevates the homemaker and her children.

In the middle of this comes this obscure phrasing in the King James Version: "Though ye have lien among the pots, yet shall ye be as the wings of a dove covered with silver, and her feathers with yellow gold." The literal rendering "lien among the pots" is ambiguous, but intriguing. The contextual thought flow gives clarity—God pours goodness upon weakness, and He elevates that which was once abased and broken. He brings peace out of tumult, strength out of weakness, prosperity out of poverty, and blessing out of suffering.

He restores flight for handicapped wings.

The sense of the "pots" phrase is this: Though sometimes we are down, out, weak, weary, or grounded. Though we lie in sheepfolds rather than flying with eagles. Though we endure boiling refining pots rather than soaring in the heavens. Though we feel pinned in spiritual battle rather than airborne in triumphant celebration. Though we experience seasons of waiting and weakness . . .

*In God's story, we all end up flying again—this time on new wings of gold and silver.*

In modern vernacular, we might say: "Though you've been down, out, and in the fire, there's coming a day where you'll be soaring on wings of gold." Though you feel like you will never fly again, flight is coming. God's going to restore your wings.

Then David says, "Thy God hath commanded thy strength: strengthen, O God, that which thou hast wrought for us" (Ps. 68:28 KJV). Think of it. Jesus has already commanded the strength you need for His work. His supply is held in reserve and is now ready for you.

It is my prayer that our time together has helped you rediscover and sustain that strength.

Hopefully, this book has given you permission to do things differently in obedience to Jesus. Lots of resources provide surface hacks, and sometimes those hacks are helpful. I'm not disparaging new methods or good ideas, but I pray this book releases you from their burden. Somebody else's great idea may not work in your context because you are not running someone else's race.

We often go at ministry in ways God never intended. We begin with the goal of outcomes and results rather than Jesus. Then we work backward, hoping for mechanics to yield the desired results. When tweaks don't work, in disappointment we seek alternative ideas. When tweaks *do* work, the results are superficial and unfulfilling because it's Jesus we crave, not results or accomplishments.

Everything changes when we finally stop chasing results and start pursuing intimacy with Jesus. Serving Him in love from spiritual fullness liberates us from the machinery and mechanics of ministry, and rests us in the beauty of Christ. He is enough, and gospel ministry is about helping people experience His wonderful enoughness. This is when *real* ministry begins.

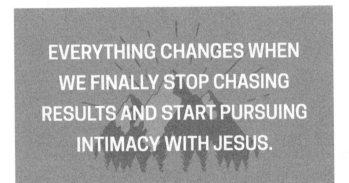

EVERYTHING CHANGES WHEN WE FINALLY STOP CHASING RESULTS AND START PURSUING INTIMACY WITH JESUS.

God's pasture is restful, joyful, and fruitful. When we let go of our constructs, cooperate with His heart, and let ministry flow from contented love for Jesus, our souls find the joy and fullness we seek. Out of this, our service is energized in surprising and delightful ways.

Tim Keller expressed this long, steady view of ministry this way, "Never, ever, ever, ever, ever think that God's not working, no matter how much it seems like He's absent; and at the same time never,

never, never, never think you're going to be able to figure out for a long time what He's up to."[1]

———

One of the things Dana and I enjoy is relaxing together with a favorite TV show. For years my friends encouraged us to watch *Downton Abbey*. I resisted. British drama is generally not my thing, but one day we were at a loss. Finally, I relented with a few conditions.

"I'm going to turn on subtitles, focus, and watch three episodes. If I'm not hooked by then, I'm out!"

I'm hesitant to admit—I was hooked. Several months and six seasons later, we watched the grand finale of all grand finales, both of us in tears. Dana was simultaneously crying at the story and laughing at me.

Then came the first *Downton Abbey* movie. I treated my wife and two daughters-in-law to a night out—three girls and Dad (my daughter was away at college).

Before the show, my mind wrestled with the present heaviness of ministry. Big, distracting challenges churned in my psyche. Moments later, the movie started, and I tried to focus on the story. Then, unexpectedly, a scene pierced through my mental fog to the heart of the issue.

Mary, a key character and evident leader of the Downton estate, was brooding in exasperation over her immense responsibilities. As she spoke to her lady's maid, Anna, she contemplated giving up the estate. She wanted out from under the incessant pressures.

At a point of brutal honesty, she asked if it was time to throw in the towel.

Anna responded with dismay, asking if this was what Mary truly wanted.

Mary released an exasperated reply that instantly put a lump in my throat: "I want everything to stop being *such a struggle*. Will the staff stay? Will the farms pay? What are we going to do about the roof? . . . What am I doing?"[2]

It wasn't lost on me that I've spent a similar decade dealing with the same issues—especially roof repairs and rain.

In that dark theater, I had been asking myself the same questions. *What am I doing? Who am I? What do I bring to this? When will everything stop being such a struggle?*

Anna's firm and insightful response to Mary is what pierced me. "I'll tell you what you're doing . . . You're making a *center* for the people who work here. For this village. For the county. Downton Abbey is the heart of this community, and you're keeping it beating."

"So you think we should battle on?" Mary asked.

"While there's blood in your veins."[3]

A healthy church is "a heart" or a center of faith for God's people—it is an outpost of hope in a dreary world. It is a garden for growth, a family for the fatherless, a strength for the weary, and a home for hearts ravaged by sin. This "heart of redemption" doesn't exist anywhere else on the planet. Your church—the church of Jesus—provides lifeblood to God's heritage, gospel light to lost hearts, and biblical foundations for future generations.

*And God chose to use you to help keep that heart beating.*

As that line dropped in the movie, tears immediately burned in my eyes. A million painful memories flashed across the pages of my mind—images of toil, stress, labor, sleepless nights, anxiety, and turmoil. Recollections of unkind people, untrue slander, and undesired storms emerged from recently buried memories.

But then the images shifted. I thought of new believers recently baptized, grade-school kids learning a biblical worldview, young adults being discipled in the ways of Jesus, and first-generation Christians building their futures and families on Jesus.

God gave immediate clarity.

*Should we continue? Shouldn't we throw in the towel?*

*While there is blood in our veins*, let us serve to keep the heart beating.

———

I want to close our time by sharing a letter. Dana and I received this when we returned from a recent summer break. Perhaps most striking about it was that its author, Amy, had just returned home from an eight-month ICU hospitalization in a near-death health battle. At the letter's writing, Amy was finally home but still weak. It had been the most difficult year of her life, and we had shed many tears with her family.

The letter was curiously attached to a large container of maple syrup.

*Dear Cary & Dana,*

*Welcome back from your time away together! Here is our gift of maple syrup to you. You are God's gift to us.*

*We love maple syrup! It's so natural and sweet. It's not fancy, and it doesn't pretend to be something else, like Log Cabin syrup does. It just delights us!*

*The beautiful sugar maple needs cold winters, like Dana does, and will only produce sap where temperatures plunge to freezing and then rise to warmth. It graciously suffers itself to be drilled into, year after year, by those needing to extract its precious sap. Then, that sap is vigorously boiled down to a sweet, dark, robust syrup, which sweetens the lives of all who taste it.*

*You are our maple syrup!*

*Thank you both for pouring yourselves into our lives. You are precious to us and are irreplaceably loved.*

*The sugar maple is extremely shade tolerant. We know that you can relate to having some shade thrown on you! And its roots are very deep. It draws water from the lower levels up toward the surface, where it expels it, benefiting the other plants around it. The story of its years is revealed in its rings. All of the bountiful years and the difficult years combine to produce a beautiful, unique tree, a gift to all around it, of so much goodness.*

*We are thankful for the Lord's goodness to us all in letting us share these ten years with you. We love you.*

*—David & Amy*

By God's grace, we can be like the sugar maple tree—rooted and grounded in Jesus, enduring the winters, renewing our resources, and always dispersing the sweetness of our Savior.

Not long ago, I stood with my two sons on a hill just above the Sea of Galilee, slightly west of Capernaum. It was the likely site of the Sermon on the Mount in Matthew's gospel. Our group opened to Matthew 5 and slowly read the Beatitudes—Jesus' formula for supreme blessedness and great joy in life.

As we close our time together, consider again the nourishing depth of Jesus' heart for our journey:

"Blessed are the *poor in spirit*, for theirs is the kingdom of heaven. Blessed are those who *mourn*, for they shall be comforted. Blessed are the *meek*, for they shall inherit the earth. Blessed are those who *hunger and thirst for righteousness*, for they shall be satisfied. Blessed are the *merciful*, for they shall receive mercy. Blessed are the *pure in heart*, for they shall see God. Blessed are the *peacemakers*, for they shall be called sons of God. Blessed are those who are *persecuted for righteousness' sake*, for theirs is the kingdom of heaven. Blessed are you when others *revile you and persecute you* and utter all kinds of evil against you falsely on my account. Rejoice and be glad, for your reward is great in heaven, for so they persecuted the prophets who were before you." (Matt. 5:3–12)

He continued . . .

"You are the *salt of the earth* . . ." (v. 13)—Don't lose the savor that the gospel and the joy of Jesus bring to your soul. Be the flavor of Jesus in a bitter, broken world.

"You are the *light of the world* . . ." (v. 14)—Don't let depletion and discouragement dim the light that lives within you. Shine audaciously and let the glory of God radiate from your heart.

As Moses prayed at the end of His life, "Let the beauty of the LORD our God be upon us: and establish thou the work of our hands . . ." (Ps. 90:17 KJV).

Thank you for serving Jesus and ministering the gospel. Thank you for embracing the intense burdens of spiritual battle. Thank you for caring well for your soul so that through you, the beauty of Jesus can radiate to others.

Keep rowing in the dark—Jesus is there, and there are more souls to feed.

Wait out the weariness—harvest is going to be spectacular.

Be willing to be "drilled into"—only sink your roots deeper in Jesus.

Don't throw in the towel—His strength is renewable.

Anticipate flying again—your new wings are coming.

Keep the heart beating. Keep the center of faith open. Keep the outpost for hope operating for those who need Jesus.

Seek Jesus first. Realize it is Him you long for. His love is better than life.

Bless Him as you live and bless others in His name. Be satisfied in Him alone.

Until we see Him, safe soaring my friend!

*For you have been my help, and in the shadow of your wings I will sing for joy. My soul clings to you; your right hand upholds me.*
Psalm 63:7–8

# APPENDIX

## Part One—Cultivate a Strong Core

*#1—Embrace Insufficiency*
*#2—Seek Jesus*
*#3—Delight in Obedience*
*#4—Celebrate Gospel Durability*
*#5—Grow a Gospel Identity*

## Part Two—Nurture a Flourishing Soul

*#1—Counterbalance Negative Flow*
*#2—Maintain a Sustainable Pace*
*#3—Pursue Body and Brain Wellness*
*#4—Nurture Healthy Relationships*
*#5—Open Up to Real Friends*
*#6—Enjoy Solitude with Jesus*

## Part Three—Lead a Healthy Culture

*#1—Teach the Word with Consistent Clarity*
*#2—Multiply Disciples in Gospel Mission*
*#3—Resist Elevation with Relatable Leadership*
*#4—Strengthen Hearts with Strong Care*

# ACKNOWLEDGMENTS

Writing a book is a daunting privilege as well as an immense team effort. This project would not have been realized without the efforts and support of an amazing group of gifted and godly people. I'm thankful beyond words to those below who profoundly influenced and contributed to these pages:

**To My Family**—Thank you for encouraging me in the ministry of writing! Dana—you not only challenged me to keep writing, but you also endured many long hours, late nights, and endless questions for feedback. Thank you for being my best friend and first listening ear. To my kids and their spouses—Lance and Hillarie, Larry and Mariah, Haylee and Cainan—thank you for your faithful support, positive words, thoughtful feedback, and creative contribution throughout the process. Lance, thanks for a great cover design!

**To the Emmanuel Ministry Team and Church Family**—Thank you to our staff and church family for supportively encouraging the writing process and for contributing to a ministry culture of health. You are my greatest friends and co-laborers, and you truly make serving Jesus a joyful, life-giving, and strengthening experience. Thank you for embracing and guarding a gospel-shaped culture.

**To My Assistant, Ashlee Dickerson**—Thank you for your endless hours of proofreading, formatting, and footnoting. Thank you for joyfully reading and rereading this manuscript many times. Your excellent input has been invaluable, and I'm grateful that you would use your gifts to bless me and others.

**To the Moody Publishers Team**—Thank you to Paul Santhouse for your invitation to partner with Moody and for your leadership. Thank you to Trillia Newbell for our early conversations in which you suggested a project for pastors and spiritual leaders. I'm grateful for our shared burden to strengthen God's servants. Thank you to Drew Dyck for your friendship, encouragement, editorial genius, and great sense of humor. It was a privilege to walk through this project with you. Thank you to Amanda Cleary Eastep for your fantastic editorial direction and input. Your insights were always brilliant. Thank you to each of the many servant-hearted people at Moody who invested time and skill to bring this book into the world. I was blessed at every point to interact and partner with you, and I'm thankful that we can serve Jesus' church together.

**To My Agent, Cynthia Ruchti**—Thank you for your friendship and your gracious and godly heart. Thank you for giving every chapter a first read and for deeply investing your time and heart into making this book better for God's servants. You are a great agent, but more so a wonderful lady with a huge heart of love and grace. I'm profoundly thankful that God brought you into my life.

# NOTES

### Chapter 1

1. *The Polar Express*, directed by Robert Zemeckis (Beverly Hills, CA: Castle Rock Entertainment, 2014).

### Chapter 2

1. Cary Schmidt, *Stop Trying: How to Receive—Not Achieve—Your Real Identity* (Chicago: Moody, 2021).

### Chapter 3

1. C. S. Lewis, "To Arthur Greeves" (December 29, 1935), in *The Collected Letters of C.S. Lewis, Volume II: Books, Broadcasts, and the War, 1931–1949*, ed. Walter Hooper (New York: HarperCollins, 2004), 174.

### Chapter 4

1. Cary Schmidt, *Off Script: What to Do When God Rewrites Your Life* (Lancaster, CA: Striving Together Publications, 2011).
2. Skip Heitzig, "John 5:31–6:21," teaching series transcript, May 25, 2016, http://skipheitzig.com/teachings_view.asp?ServiceID=4076&transcript=1#transcript.

## Chapter 5

1. Homer, *The Odyssey*, Book XII.
2. "Slipstream," Wikipedia, last modified May 17, 2023, https:// en.wikipedia.org/wiki/Slipstream.
3. Martin E.P. Seligman, *Learned Optimism: How to Change Your Mind and Your Life* (New York: Vintage Books, 2006).
4. Augustine of Hippo, "Lectures or Tractates on the Gospel According to St. John," in *St. Augustine: Homilies on the Gospel of John; Homilies on the First Epistle of John; Soliloquies*, A Select Library of the Nicene and Post-Nicene Fathers of the Christian Church, vol. 7, ed. Philip Schaff, trans. John Gibb and James Innes (New York: Christian Literature Company, 1888), 90.
5. J. C. Ryle, "Commentary on John 3" (v. 30 under "Notes"), *Ryle's Expository Thoughts on the Gospels*, https://www.studylight.org/ commentaries/eng/ryl/john-3.html.

## Chapter 6

1. W. M. Malcolm, E. A. Fisher and E. Prusaczyk, "The Complexity of Assessing Ministry-Specific Satisfaction and Stress," *Journal of Psychology and Theology* 50, no. 3 (2021): 320–39, https://journals.sagepub .com/doi/10.1177/00916471211021921.

## Chapter 7

1. Martin E. P. Seligman, *Learned Optimism: How to Change Your Mind and Your Life* (New York: Vintage Books, 2006).
2. Stephen R. Covey, A. Roger Merrill, and Rebecca R. Merrill, *First Things First* (Miami, FL: Mango Media, 2015), 96–97 of 418, Scribd.
3. Ibid., 123 of 418, Scribd.

## Chapter 8

1. Eric Suni, "How Much Sleep Do We Really Need?," Sleep Foundation, updated May 9, 2023, https://www.sleepfoundation.org/ how-sleep-works/how-much-sleep-do-we-really-need.

2. Simon Sinek, *Leaders Eat Last: Why Some Teams Pull Together and Others Don't* (New York: Portfolio/Penguin, 2017).

3. Ibid., 52–54.

4. Ibid., 54–55.

5. Ibid., 60–63.

6. Ibid., 63–65.

7. Ibid., 68–74.

8. Mayo Clinic Staff, "Chronic Stress Puts Your Health at Risk," Mayo Clinic, July 8, 2021, https://www.mayoclinic.org/healthy-lifestyle/stress-management/in-depth/stress/art-20046037.

9. Cleveland Clinic, "Cortisol," https://my.clevelandclinic.org/health/articles/22187-cortisol.

## Chapter 9

1. *Peanuts* (comic series), created by Charles Schulz (New York: Peanuts Worldwide LLC, original run 1950–2000).

2. The thoughts explored in this section on stress were heavily informed by a series of personal and recorded conversations with my friend Dr. Jonathan Hoover, Associate Pastor and Couples Pastor at NewSpring Church in Wichita, Kansas, and a professor of psychology at Regent University. Jonathan has been featured several times on my podcast, *Leading in the Gospel,* as we explored the topics of soul health in ministry leaders. His insight and counsel regarding stress management have been very helpful to me, and I'm happy to pass it on in these pages. You can benefit from Jonathan's ministry by starting here: jonathanhoover.online, and you would be encouraged by listening to my podcast episodes with Jonathan at inthegospel.com/podcast (also available on Apple Podcasts, Spotify, and Google Podcasts).

3. Brad A. Roy, "Overreaching/Overtraining: More Is Not Always Better," *ACSM's Health & Fitness Journal* 19, no. 2 (April 2015): 4, https://doi.org/10.1249/FIT.0000000000000100.

## Chapter 10

1. *14 Peaks: Nothing Is Impossible* (documentary), directed by Torquil Jones (Los Gatos, CA: Netflix, Inc., 2021).
2. Ibid.
3. Dictionary.com, s.v. "grandiosity," https://www.dictionary.com/browse/grandiosity.
4. Michael O'Donnell, "'The Extraordinary Life of an Ordinary Man' Review: Paul Newman's Verdict," *Wall Street Journal*, October 15, 2022, https://www.wsj.com/articles/the-extraordinary-life-of-an-ordinary-man-review-paul-newmans-verdict-11665835203.
5. Arthur C. Brooks, *From Strength to Strength: Finding Success, Happiness, and Deep Purpose in the Second Half of Life* (New York: Portfolio/Penguin, 2022), 129–32.

## Chapter 11

1. There are conflicting opinions of which Dionysius this story is attributed to in the writing of Cicero—whether Dionysius the First or Second. Given the conflicting accounts, we chose to leave the structure as is in this retelling.
2. *Encyclopaedia Britannica*, s.v. "Damocles," https://www.britannica.com/topic/Damocles.
3. Evan Andrews, "What Was the Sword of Damocles?," History.com, updated August 23, 2018, https://www.history.com/news/what-was-the-sword-of-damocles.
4. Cicero, "Book V: Whether Virtue Alone Be Sufficient for a Happy Life" (XX–XXIII), *Cicero's Tusculan Disputations*, trans. C. D. Yonge (New York: Harper & Brothers, Publishers, 1877), 184–86, https://www.gutenberg.org/files/14988/14988-h/14988-h.htm.
5. Kevin A. Miller, *Secret of Staying Power: Overcoming the Discouragements of Ministry* (Carol Stream, IL: Christianity Today, Inc., 1988), 108 of 121, Scribd.
6. Ibid., 23 of 121, Scribd.
7. Elton Trueblood, *While It Is Day: An Autobiography* (New York: Harper & Row, 1974), 67.

8. Christina Maslach and Susan E. Jackson, "The Measurement of Experienced Burnout," *Journal of Organizational Behavior* 2, no. 2 (April 1981): 99–113, https://doi.org/10.1002/job.4030020205.

9. Again, this section on burnout flows initially from multiple conversations with Dr. Jonathan Hoover over a period of six years. It was Jonathan's influence that sparked my further interest and research into the experience of burnout, with a desire to avoid and help others to avoid the phenomenon. Jonathan's counsel and personal encouragement have proven very insightful in my journey, and this section would not be what it is without his thumbprint.

10. Rodger Charlton et al., "Clergy Work-Related Psychological Health: Listening to the Ministers of Word and Sacrament Within the United Reformed Church in England," *Pastoral Psychology* 58 (April 2009): 133–49, https://doi.org/10.1007/s11089-008-0177-3.

11. Cary Schmidt, *Enough for Today* (recorded and produced in Newington, CT: Emmanuel Baptist Church), https://ebcnewington.com/enoughfortoday.

12. John Piper, "Embrace the Life God Has Given You," Desiring God, March 10, 2017, https://www.desiringgod.org/embrace-the-life-god-has-given-you.

13. As quoted by Alexandra Michel, "Burnout and the Brain," *APS Observer*, January 29, 2016, https://www.psychologicalscience.org/observer/burnout-and-the-brain. This article cites "For the Young Doctor About to Burn Out," by Richard Gunderman, which gives a variation of this quote: "Professional burnout is the sum total of hundreds and thousands of tiny betrayals of purpose, each one so minute that it hardly attracts notice": Richard Gunderman, "For the Young Doctor About to Burn Out," *Atlantic*, February 21, 2014, https://www.theatlantic.com/health/archive/2014/02/for-the-young-doctor-about-to-burn-out/284005/.

## Chapter 12

1. Charles Spurgeon, *An All-Around Ministry: Addresses to Ministers and Students* (New York: Scriptura Press, 2015), 45–46 of 381, Scribd.

2. Matthew 5:15 KJV.

3. Patrick Lencioni, *The Motive: Why So Many Leaders Abdicate Their Most Important Responsibilities* (Hoboken, NJ: John Wiley & Sons, Inc., 2020), 135–39.

4. Ibid., 114.

5. Ray Ortlund, "Ray Ortlund on Renewal for Tired Pastors," *The Gospel Coalition* (podcast), April 23, 2021, 44:35, https://www.thegospelcoalition.org/podcasts/tgc-podcast/ray-ortlund-on-renewal-for-tired-pastors.

## Conclusion

1. Timothy Keller (@timkellernyc), "Never, ever, ever, ever, ever think that God's not working, no matter how much it seems like He's absent; and at the same time never, never, never, never think you're going to be able to figure out for a long time what He's up to," Twitter, October 3, 2022, 7:11 a.m., https://twitter.com/timkellernyc/status/1576892568985534465.

2. "Downton Abbey (2019) Transcript," *TV Show Transcripts*, written by Julian Fellowes, https://tvshowtranscripts.ourboard.org/viewtopic.php?f=150&t=36077.

3. Ibid.